Using Money

Level 3 – Level 5

JANE ELLIS
LUCY PODDINGTON

CONTENTS

Introduction — 3

Unit 1: Value of Money

Level 3	5
Level 4	12
Level 5	21
Generic Sheets	28

Unit 2: Calculating

Level 3	32
Level 4	40
Level 5	50
Generic Sheets	58

Unit 3: Prices

Level 3	65
Level 4	73
Level 5	83
Generic Sheets	90

Pupil Assessment Sheet — 96

Published by Hopscotch Educational Publishing Ltd, 29 Waterloo Place, Leamington Spa CV32 5LA. (Tel: 01926 744227)

© 2002 Hopscotch Educational Publishing Ltd

Produced for Hopscotch Educational Publishing Ltd by Bender Richardson White, Uxbridge

Devised and planned by Jane Ellis

Activity sheets created by Lucy Poddington

Edited by Lionel Bender

Page make-up and illustration by Pumpkin House, Cambridge

Cover illustrated by Susan Hutchison

Printed by Stephens and George Ltd

Jane Ellis and Lucy Poddington hereby assert their moral right to be identified as the authors of this work in accordance with the Copyright, Designs and Patents Act, 1988.

National Numeracy Strategy Framework for Teaching © Crown copyright March 1999

ISBN 1-904307-01-9

All rights reserved. This book is sold subject to the condition that it shall not, by way of trade or otherwise, be lent, hired out or otherwise circulated without the publisher's prior consent in any form of binding or cover other than that in which it is published and without a similar condition, including this condition, being imposed upon the subsequent purchaser.

No part of this publication may be reproduced, stored in a retrieval system, or transmitted, in any form or by any means, electronic, mechanical, photocopying, recording or otherwise, without the prior permission of the publisher, except where photocopying for the educational establishment that has purchased this book is expressly permitted in the text.

INTRODUCTION

ABOUT THE SERIES

Using Classroom Resources is a series of books that provides teachers with lessons using available resources such as money and clocks. While the lessons and activities are taught in line with the requirements of The National Numeracy Strategy's *Framework for teaching*, there are many additional ideas and activities that enable teachers to broaden the work.

These books are ideal because they offer considerable practice for those children who are struggling to grasp the concepts and skills, while also providing extension activities for those children who have grasped the concepts and skills.

The books are organised into three sections which relate to different aspects of the subject. Within each section are lesson plans and photocopiable activities for the different levels of ability being addressed. At the end of each section are generic sheets that can be used in a variety of ways.

The learning objectives in the series have been linked closely to the National Numeracy Strategy's Framework and the introduction to each level has a strong emphasis on whole-class direct teaching as well as a planned purposeful plenary. Teachers should select from the range of activities given in each level in order to differentiate the work for the ability of their class.

Display ideas are included at the end of each level to help the teacher promote continuous learning through the classroom environment.

ABOUT THIS BOOK

This book aims to:
- provide clear lesson plans that focus on specific learning objectives linked to the children's yearly teaching programme
- support teachers through activity ideas based on whole-class, group, paired and individual learning
- help the children to understand the value of money in real-life situations, for example pocket money and household bills
- give the children many opportunities to handle coins and notes and use them in role play
- produce fun activities to help the children appreciate the value of money
- encourage the children to be confident in the life-long skills of totalling prices and calculating change.

LINKS TO THE CURRICULUM

This book contains activities that are organised into the levels that relate to the National Curriculum level descriptions. The expectations in the yearly teaching programmes correspond to these levels:

Year 3: Level 3
Year 4: Revision of Level 3, Level 4
Year 5: Revision of Level 4, start on Level 5
Year 6: Level 5

Content of the National Numeracy Strategy's Framework for Yearly Teaching Programmes
Following are the links to the 'Solving problems' strand of the Framework.

Year 3
- Solve word problems involving money, using one or more steps, including finding totals and giving change, and working out which coins to pay.
- Explain how the problem was solved.
- Recognise all coins and notes.
- Understand and use £.p notation (for example, know that £3.06 is £3 and 6p).

Year 4
- Use all four operations to solve word problems involving money, using one or more steps, including converting pound to pence and vice versa.

Year 5
- Use all four operations to solve simple word problems involving money, using one or more steps, including making simple conversions of pounds Sterling to foreign currency and finding simple percentages.
- Explain methods and reasoning.

Year 6
- Identify and use appropriate operations (including combinations of operations) to solve word problems involving money, using one or more steps, including converting pounds Sterling to foreign currency, or vice versa, and calculating percentages such as VAT.
- Explain methods and reasoning.

These are the expectations for each year group. Skills need to be practised continuously and, therefore, there may be assessment of pre-requisite knowledge in each yearly teaching programme. For example, some objectives from Years 4 and 5 would continue to be assessed in Year 6.

▶ Introduction

🕐 Learning objectives

The learning objectives give a clear teaching focus for each unit. It is good practice to display and share the learning objectives with the children at the beginning of each lesson.

🕐 Key vocabulary

The majority of the words have been taken from the NNS Mathematical Vocabulary book. Ideally these words should also be displayed, and referred to, during the lesson. If there are children with language difficulties, it can be effective to point at the words as they are used.

🕐 Resources

This list is only a suggestion of resources that may be used by the children or teacher. These resources, and others, should be readily available in school.

🕐 Introduction

This outlines how you could introduce and teach the topics and skills the children need to learn in the unit. The emphasis is on whole-class teaching and creating interactive activities through direct teaching.

The direct teaching methods outlined in the National Numeracy Strategy's Framework are:
- directing
- instructing
- demonstrating
- explaining and illustrating
- questioning and discussing
- consolidating
- evaluating the children's responses
- summarising.

🕐 Activity sheets

The activity sheets provide tasks which the children can do more or less independently from the teacher. They are designed to support and reinforce teaching, not replace it. Before the children are given the activity sheets to work on, the teacher should ensure that the whole class has understood the numeracy principles being tested. The notes introducing each activity sheet give ideas and suggestions for making the most of the sheets. They sometimes make suggestions for the whole-class introduction, the plenary session or follow-up work based on the activity sheet.

🕐 Support

Here are ideas for simplifying the tasks to enable lower-attaining children to have access to the learning objectives. They may involve adapting the activity sheet or one of the generic sheets, using numbers appropriate to the level of attainment.

🕐 Challenge

Here are ideas to extend the content of the activity sheets for higher-attaining children.

🕐 Plenary

These are carefully planned activities to finish a lesson, through reflection and assessment. To be effective, there should be a 10 to 15 minutes' time allowance at the end of the lesson. The emphasis again is on whole-class, interactive teaching. It is good practice to refer back to the learning objective and ask 'What have you learned today?'

🕐 Display opportunity

These ideas will enable the teacher to transfer work from the lesson on to a display board. Children continue to learn through displays, and many suggestions in this book include interactive displays where the teacher can continue to 'teach' through changing questions on the wall.

🕐 Extra activities

Here are additional ideas to help the children achieve the learning objectives. More suggestions are given for adapting and using the activity and generic sheets, but as teachers you will no doubt think of many more!

Value of Money: Level 3

UNIT 1: VALUE OF MONEY
LEVEL 3

Learning objectives

- To recognise all coins and notes.
- To understand and use £.p notation (for example, know that £6.02 means £6 and 2p).
- To understand how to keep a financial record.

Key vocabulary

- money, coin, note, pence, pound, £, amount, value, credit, debit, balance, cheap, expensive

Resources

- toy money (see Generic Sheet 1, page 28: copy on to stiff card, cut out the coins and notes, then glue heads/tails or front/reverse back to back)

Introduction

- Check that the children are confident with £.p notation, for example £2.12, £4.35. Write some amounts on the board in pounds and ask the children to write them in pence. Then reverse the activity. Include amounts involving zeros, such as 70p = £0.70 and 808p = £8.08.

- Revise similarities and differences between £5, £10 and £20 notes and ensure the children can recognise their values. Ask them to suggest coins or notes with an equal value to each of the notes, for example five £1 coins equal one £5 note, and two £5 notes equal one £10 note.

- Talk about why it is important to keep money safe in a bank account and to keep a record of how much money is there. Discuss how to fill in an accounts sheet. Introduce the vocabulary 'credit' (money going in), 'debit' (money going out) and 'balance' (running total). Draw columns on the board headed 'Date', 'Item', 'Credit', 'Debit' and 'Balance' and fill them in together for transactions such as pocket money going in and purchases going out. Emphasise that credit involves adding and debit involves subtracting. Ask questions based on the completed chart, for example 'What was the most expensive item bought?', 'When was the largest amount of money in the account?' and 'How much money was credited in total?'

Activities

- **Activity Sheet 1** – Organise the children into pairs and give each pair one copy of the sheet and a small opaque bag for the cards. Remind them of the word 'value' and explain that £2 has the same value as, or is equal to, 200p. Explain that on some turns both children will be able to cross their grids, on others just one child will, and on some turns neither child will. Ask them to cross the grids in pencil so that the crosses can be erased and the game can be played again. The winner is the first to cross out all the values on their grid.

- **Activity Sheet 2** – This activity provides practice in recognising the value of notes and coins and using £.p notation. Ensure that the children count all the pounds first and then add the pence. Ask them to check that they have written the digits in the correct decimal place, for example £5 and 3 pence is £5.03, not £5.3 or £5.30. Encourage them to practise exchanging notes for other notes or coins of equivalent value, using the money on Generic Sheet 1 (page 28). This will help to reinforce the value of the notes.

- **Activity Sheet 3** – Use this with the cards on Generic Sheet 2 (page 29). Organise the children into pairs. Revise the vocabulary 'credit', 'debit' and 'balance' and explain that an accounts sheet or bank statement usually starts with an 'opening balance', which is how much money is already in the account. The 'closing balance' is how much money is in the account at the end. Explain that they will need to decide whether each card shows a credit (money going in) or a debit (money going out). Clues are provided in words such as 'buy', 'save', 'give' and 'earn'. When they have completed the activity sheet using a random selection of eight cards, they can check that their calculations are correct: the opening balance plus the total credit minus the total debit should equal the closing balance. The

▶ **Value of Money: Level 3**

activity can be repeated using another copy of the sheet (a different set of cards will be picked each time, leading to a different accounts sheet). Ask the children to draw up their own accounts sheet for homework, showing how much pocket money they receive and what they spend it on, over the course of one or two weeks.

- **Activity Sheet 4** – This activity encourages the children to consider the value of money in relation to things that can be bought in a supermarket. Revise the vocabulary 'value', 'cheap', 'expensive', 'costs more', 'costs less'. Look at the items pictured and discuss which might be the cheapest and which the most expensive items. Ask them to think about whether the smallest item is necessarily the cheapest and whether largest is the most expensive. They should complete the activity in pairs and number the items in pencil so that they can change the order as many times as they wish before making their final decision. They can find out actual prices for the items as a homework activity or by visiting a supermarket website where goods can be ordered online. Alternatively, prepare a list of prices before the lesson for them to look at once they have completed the sheet.

- **Activity Sheet 5** – Read the instructions with the children and make sure they understand that they should not count all the coins, but should instead look at the coins and notes as a group and say roughly how much they think there is. You could give them prices close to the amount pictured and ask if they think there is enough money in the pile to pay the price. Discuss strategies for estimating; suggest that they look for the notes and largest coins in the pile and work out how much they are worth altogether, and use this as the basis of their estimate. Coins worth less than 50p should not be counted individually. Once they have completed the sheet, they can count the money in each pile and see how close their estimate was by finding the difference. Encourage them to discuss in pairs how they made their estimates. The children could set more questions like this for a partner to estimate, using piles of coins and notes.

Support

For Activity Sheet 3, give the children a smaller number of cards to work with (four or five) and write on each one 'credit (+)' or 'debit (–)' so that it is clear how they should record them on the accounts sheet.

Use Generic Sheet 3 (page 30) for simple matching games involving amounts in pence and amounts in pounds, or for practice in putting amounts of money in order of value. To make the cards more durable, copy them on to card and laminate them. Ask the children to work in pairs or small groups. They should take turns to pick a card and find another card which shows a matching value. Several different games can be played using the cards, for example 'Snap' or a memory game (the cards are spread face down on the table; children take it in turns to turn over two cards. If they match, the child keeps them; if not, the cards are turned back over).

Challenge

Write some amounts greater than £10 in pence, for example 1090p and 1345p, and ask the children to write them in pounds. Then reverse the activity.

When the children have completed Activity Sheet 4, ask them to write Sally's till receipt using the actual prices they found. To find the total, they could add three or four prices at a time, then add together these sub-totals to give the grand total.

Plenary

Play a credit and debit activity to reinforce that credit involves addition and debit involves subtraction. Give the children small whiteboards or scrap paper for recording their workings. Begin with an 'opening balance' such as £5 and read out a series of credits and debits, for example 'Credit £2.75. Debit £1.30...' Ask them to record the total after each addition or subtraction and the final total, or 'closing balance'.

Display opportunity

Make a chart for display with two columns headed 'Credit' and 'Debit'. Ask the children to suggest different types of credit (such as earnings, prize winnings, birthday money) and debit (such as purchases, donations to charity, household bills, membership fees). Write their ideas on the display.

Name_____   ▸ Value of Money – Activity Sheet 1

Money bingo

Cut out the cards below and put them in a bag.

Write your name on a grid. With your partner, take the cards out of the bag one by one. If you can find the same value on your grid, cross it out.

Who crosses out all their values first?

Name:_____

£9.90	495p	£1.01
531p	£3.30	710p
£1.10	1000p	£0.80

Name:_____

£3.90	100p	£1.99
1000p	£0.55	662p
£1.01	710p	£3.30

101p	199p	£7.10	110p	£1.00
330p	£5.31	303p	£10.00	£4.95
55p	80p	£6.62	990p	390p

PHOTOCOPIABLE
© Hopscotch Educational Publishing 2002

Name_____   ▶ Value of Money – Activity Sheet 2

Value of notes

Write the total value in pounds and pence.

For example, £12.40.

total _____

total _____

total _____

total _____

total _____

total _____

total _____

total _____

Name_____   ▸ Value of Money – Activity Sheet 3

Credit and debit

Mix up the accounts sheet cards and spread them out face down.

With a friend, pick eight cards. Record the credits and debits on the accounts sheet. Work out the balance after each credit or debit.

Write the closing balance at the end.

Write the dates in the correct order.

Date	Item	Credit (+)	Debit (−)	Balance
Accounts sheet — Opening balance: £10.00				
Closing balance:				

Work out the total amount credited. _____

Work out the total amount debited. _____

PHOTOCOPIABLE
© Hopscotch Educational Publishing 2002

Supermarket values

Sally has been to the supermarket. Estimate which items were cheap and which were expensive. Number the items in order of value from 1 (cheapest) to 10 (most expensive).

Which items do you think cost more than £3?

_____

How much might Sally's total bill be? Tick the best estimate.

£15   £30   £50

Find out actual supermarket prices for the items Sally bought. Compare your estimates with the actual prices.

Name_____   ▸ Value of Money – Activity Sheet 5

Estimating money

How much money do you think there is in each box? Write an estimate.

"Don't count all the coins. Just estimate!"

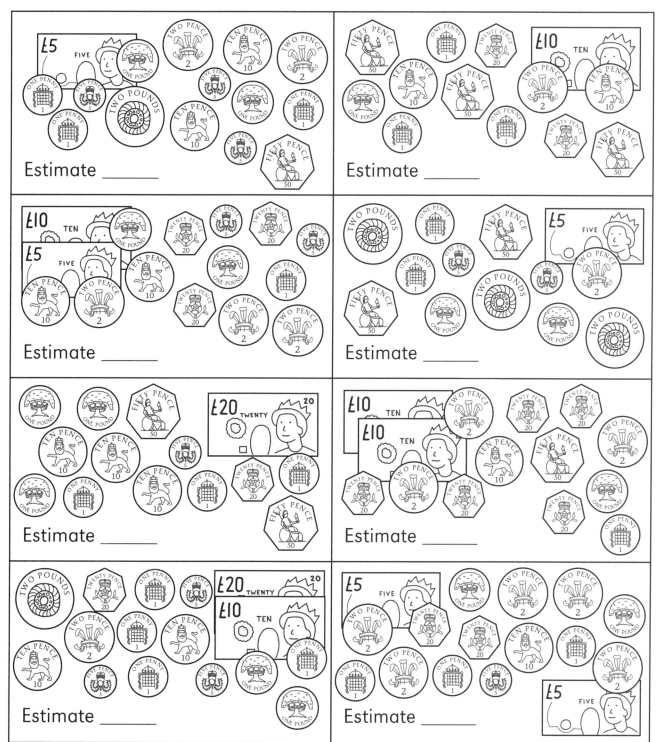

Value of Money: Level 4

UNIT 1: VALUE OF MONEY
LEVEL 4

Learning objectives

- To convert pounds to pence and vice versa.
- To convert pounds to foreign currency.
- To solve problems involving money.
- To appreciate the value of money in real-life situations.

Key vocabulary

- amount, value, currency, fixed charge, direct debit

Resources

- enlarged copies of household bills
- calculators

Introduction

- Practise converting pounds to pence and vice versa. Include amounts greater than £10, such as 1023p = £10.23 and 2890p = £28.90.
- Introduce the word 'currency' and talk to the children about different currencies they may have handled whilst on holiday, such as euros or US dollars. Discuss which European countries use the euro. Tell them how many euros are equal in value to £1 and explain that this is called the 'exchange rate'.
- Introduce the value of money in relation to regular household expenses, such as gas, electricity and telephone bills. Discuss what we use gas and electricity for in the home and what other regular expenses there are. Make a list together. Show the children an enlarged copy of a gas or electricity bill and explain how it is calculated, i.e. the meter is read and the number of units used is multiplied by the price per unit. Explain the 'fixed charge' or 'standing charge' and the VAT of 5%. Introduce the term 'direct debit' and talk about the advantages and disadvantages of paying bills by monthly direct debit.

Activities

- **Activity Sheet 6** – Revise how to convert pounds to pence and vice versa. Reinforce that converting pounds to pence is the same as multiplying by 100 (moving the digits two places to the left) and that converting pence to pounds is the same as dividing by 100 (moving the digits two places to the right).

- **Activity Sheet 7** – Encourage the children to calculate carefully and to make sure that they compare the two amounts in the same unit (either pence or pounds). Ask them to correct any false statements. They could set more questions like this for a partner to solve. It will be helpful if they first write out how many of each coin are needed to make certain amounts, for example £20 is 2000 x 1p or 1000 x 2p or 400 x 5p and so on.

- **Activity Sheet 8** – This activity helps the children to appreciate the value of money in relation to things that can be bought. Provide a range of newspaper advertisements and supplements, shop catalogues and so on relevant to the items on the sheet.

- **Activity Sheet 9** – This activity could link with work in history on Britain since 1948. If possible, show the children examples of pre-1971 coins, notes and stamps so that they can compare them with present-day money. Explain that the shilling was replaced by the new 5p coin, and the large old pennies were replaced by new pennies (worth more than the old ones). When they have completed the sheet, ask them to explain how they worked out the answers. Talk about question 4 and how prices have risen since 1965. If appropriate, introduce the term 'inflation'.

- **Activity Sheet 10** – This helps the children to understand that different currencies are used around the world, but that we can find equivalent values in different currencies by looking at exchange rates. Emphasise that the items on the chart have the same value whether they are paid for in pounds, euros or US dollars. Before beginning the activity, revise how to round numbers with two decimal places to the nearest whole number. Decide whether or not to let the children use calculators.

▶ **Value of Money: Level 4**

- **Activity Sheet 11** – Look at the bills on the activity sheet and point out that some bills arrive annually (once a year), some quarterly (every three months) and others every month. Revise the vocabulary 'direct debit', 'fixed charge' and 'VAT'. Explain why there is a difference in the amount of VAT paid on fuel bills and other bills such as telephone bills. Revise how to find percentages and show them how to calculate 5% by finding 10% and then halving it. Show them how to use calculators to find 17.5%. During the plenary, discuss why the Arnold family might not in fact pay the amount per year that the children have calculated (the gas and electricity bills will vary throughout the year according to how much heating is needed in the home).

- **Activity Sheet 12** – This activity introduces the children to budgeting for real-life situations involving money. Read the brochure page with the children and introduce the word 'discount'. Discuss that to find the cottage price for two weeks it does not matter whether they subtract 10% and then double, or double and then subtract 10%. Encourage them to explain their methods to a partner. During the plenary, list all the different 'extra costs' that may need to be considered when planning a holiday, such as airport tax, flight supplements, spending money, airport parking, car hire and so on.

Support

For Activity Sheet 10, ask the children to convert to just one foreign currency (either euros or US dollars). Suggest that they round the exchange rate to £1 = 1.5 euros/US dollars, to make the calculations less challenging.

For Activity Sheet 11, fill in the VAT amounts on the bills so that the children do not need to calculate the percentages.

Challenge

Bring in a selection of objects from the house and garden (or collect pictures from magazines and catalogues). Organise the children into groups and ask them to estimate how much each item costs in a shop. Then show them a list of the actual prices, or ask them to find out using store catalogues. Points could be awarded to the group whose estimate was closest to the actual price.

Plenary

Write some realistic amounts on the board for the household bills for one year. Ask the children to work out how much is paid each month and write their answers on a piece of paper or a small whiteboard. Make sure the calculations can be done using pencil and paper procedures, or let the children use calculators.

Display opportunity

Display a picture of a house beneath the heading 'Household expenses'. Invite the children to suggest all the different expenses involved in running a house, such as mortgage or rent payments, gas and electricity bills, insurance and so on. Write them in bubbles around the house picture.

Extra activities

For more practice in rounding amounts of money, give the children the cards on Generic Sheet 3 (page 30). Ask them to pick a card and round it to the nearest pound. This will help them to realise that rounding an amount in pence to the nearest pound is the same as rounding to the nearest 100, and rounding an amount in pounds is the same as rounding to the nearest whole number.

Answers

Activity Sheet 7

| 1. True | 2. True | 3. False | 4. False |
| 5. False | 6. True | 7. False | 8. True |

Activity Sheet 9

1. a) 36   b) 60   c) 72   d) 108
2. 240
3. a) 40   b) 65   c) 75   d) 95
4. Approx. 13p, approx 9p, approx. £2.50

Activity Sheet 10

Socks	3.2 euros	2.8 US$
Hat	8 euros	7 US$
T-shirt	16 euros	14 US$
Bag	4.8 euros	4.2 US$
Gloves	6.4 euros	5.6 US$
Jumper	24 euros	21 US$
Tie	12.8 euros	11.2 US$
Scarf	9.6 euros	8.4 US$

Activity Sheet 11

1. £75
2. £6   £126   £42
3. £3.50   £73.50   £24.50
4. £10.50   £70.50   £23.50
5. £165
6. £1980

Activity Sheet 12

a) £520.50   b) £801   c) £873
The family could stay in Holly or Poppy Cottage.

Converting money

Write these amounts in pence.

_____ _____ _____ _____

_____ _____ _____ _____

Write these amounts in pounds.

_____ _____ _____ _____

_____ _____ _____ _____

Write in pence:

£100 _____   £5000 _____   £1500 _____

Write in pounds:

50000p _____   16000p _____   250000p _____

Name_____ ▸ Value of Money – Activity Sheet 7

True or false?

Decide whether each statement is true or false.
Tick thumbs up or thumbs down.

1 100 x  is less than 50 x .

2 40 x is the same as 20 x .

3 1000 x  is more than 200 x .

4 20 x  is less than 90 x .

5 50 x is the same as 250 x .

6 2500 x  is more than 40 x .

7 40 x  is more than 2000 x .

8 200 x is less than 5000 x .

PHOTOCOPIABLE
© Hopscotch Educational Publishing 2002

Name_____   ▸ Value of Money – Activity Sheet 8

What's the cost?

How much might these things cost? Tick the best estimate.

Then find out an actual price from a catalogue, newspaper or the Internet, or ask an adult. Did you estimate correctly?

A brand new car

Estimate:
£100   £1000   £10 000

Actual price: _____

A tank full of petrol

Estimate:
£5   £30   £100

Actual price: _____

A house

Estimate:
£1000   £10 000   £100 000

Actual price: _____

A kettle

Estimate:
£10   £30   £100

Actual price: _____

A trolley full of supermarket shopping
Estimate:
£15   £30   £60

Actual price: _____

A takeaway meal for four people

Estimate:
£10   £20   £50

Actual price: _____

A flight to Amsterdam

Estimate:
£100   £500   £1000

Actual price: _____

A telephone

Estimate:
£25   £100   £250

Actual price: _____

PHOTOCOPIABLE
© Hopscotch Educational Publishing 2002

Name_____   ▸ Value of Money – Activity Sheet 9

Old money

The money system in Britain changed in 1971. Before then, people used pounds, shillings and old pence.

There were 20 shillings in one pound.

There were 12d (old pence) in one shilling.

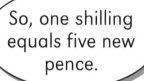

So, one shilling equals five new pence.

Answer the questions.

1 How many old pence were there in:

a) 3 shillings? _____   b) 5 shillings? _____

c) 6 shillings? _____   d) 9 shillings? _____

2 How many old pence were there in one pound? _____

3 One shilling equals five new pence. How many new pence in:

a) 8 shillings? _____   b) 13 shillings? _____

c) 15 shillings? _____   d) 19 shillings? _____

4 In 1965...

...Wendy bought a book for 2 shillings and 6d. What is this in new pence? _____

...Robert went to the cinema for 1 shilling and 9d. What is this in new pence? _____

...Pam bought some shoes for 49 shillings and 11d. What is this in pounds and new pence? _____

Give approximate answers.

17

PHOTOCOPIABLE
© Hopscotch Educational Publishing 2002

Name_____ ▸ Value of Money – Activity Sheet 10

Foreign currency

Work out approximately how much these things cost in euros and US dollars. First round up or down to the nearest pound.

Exchange rates

£1 = 1.6 euros

£1 = 1.4 US dollars

Don't forget that £0.50 rounds <u>up</u>.

Item	Price	Rounded price	Price in euros	Price in US dollars
Socks	£1.99			
Hat	£4.80			
T-shirt	£9.50			
Bag	£3.20			
Gloves	£4.45			
Jumper	£14.99			
Tie	£8.40			
Scarf	£6.25			

PHOTOCOPIABLE
© Hopscotch Educational Publishing 2002

Name_____   ▸ Value of Money – Activity Sheet 11

Household bills

Mr and Mrs Arnold have decided to pay their bills by direct debit, every month. Complete the bills to show how much they will pay.

1 Council tax bill
   £900 per year
   Monthly payment = _____

VAT is charged on the total of these two amounts.

2 Gas bill   for 3 months
   Gas used   £110.00
   Fixed charge   £10.00
   VAT @ 5% on £120.00   _____
   Total charges (for 3 months)   _____
              Monthly payment =   _____

3 Electricity bill   for 3 months
   Electricity used   £57.00
   Fixed charge   £13.00
   VAT @ 5% on £70.00   _____
   Total charges (for 3 months)   _____
              Monthly payment =   _____

4 Telephone bill   for 3 months
   Calls made   £35.00
   Fixed charge   £25.00
   VAT @ 17.5% on £60.00   _____
   Total charges (for 3 months)   _____
              Monthly payment =   _____

5 How much do they pay in total each month? _____

6 How much might they pay in a whole year? _____

Name_____   ▸ Value of Money – Activity Sheet 12

Plan a holiday

Meet the Briggs family. They are planning a holiday.

Read the brochure.

The Briggs family
2 adults
3 children

Holly Cottage £350 per week	Extra costs (no discount)
Poppy Cottage £390 per week	Heating: £25 per cottage per week
Ivy Cottage £435 per week	Parking: £8 per cottage per week
10% discount on cottage price if you stay for two weeks!	Insurance: Adult £15 per week Child £7.50 per week

How much would these holidays cost in total for the Briggs family? Show your workings.

a) One week in Ivy Cottage

b) Two weeks in Holly Cottage

c) Two weeks in Poppy Cottage

The Briggs family decide to go for one week. They want to spend less than £500. Which cottage (or cottages) could they stay in?

_____

Value of Money: Level 5

UNIT 1: VALUE OF MONEY
LEVEL 5

Learning objectives

- To convert pounds to foreign currency, or vice versa.
- To solve problems involving money.
- To appreciate the value of money in real-life situations and to begin to understand the concept of credit.

Key vocabulary

- amount, value, currency, credit, debit, hire purchase

Resources

- toy money (see Generic Sheet 1, page 28: copy on to stiff card, cut out the coins and notes, then glue heads/tails or front/reverse back to back)
- credit and debit cards

Introduction

- Ask what the children know about the euro and in which countries it is used. Calculate some currency conversions together, for example converting £200 into euros. Talk about why a single currency has been introduced in these countries and what advantages and disadvantages the single currency might have. If possible, show the children some euro notes and coins. Explain that each country has chosen a different design for the reverse of the coins, but that all the coins can be used in any country. (More information about the euro, including pictures of the notes and coins, can be found on the European Central Bank website at www.euro.ecb.int/en.html.)
- Review the meanings of the words 'credit' and 'debit'. Ask the children if they can explain what a credit card is and how it works. Discuss the advantages and disadvantages of using a credit card and list them on a chart on the board. Show them examples of credit cards and debit cards. Discuss how debit cards can be used, including for receiving cashback when paying for goods.

Activities

- **Activity Sheet 13** – The instruction on this activity sheet could be changed to show the up-to-date value of the euro at the time the sheet is used. Ask the children to round amounts in pence involving decimals, for example 10 euro cents = 6p (not 6.1p). They could use calculators for the second part of the activity. Where appropriate, encourage them to calculate using answers they have already worked out, for example multiplying the value of a 10 euro note by two to find the value of a 20 euro note.

- **Activity Sheet 14** – The children will need to look in newspapers or on the Internet to find out exchange rates. (An online currency converter can be found at www.xe.com/ucc/.) Encourage them to round the exchange rates as necessary to make the numbers easier to work with (to one or two decimal places, depending on their level of attainment). When they have completed the activity, discuss the fact that the value of goods varies around the world, for example petrol is much cheaper in many countries than it is in Britain.

- **Activity Sheet 15** – This activity could link with work in history on Britain since 1948. Discuss the value of money in relation to the concept of inflation: ask the children to think about what happens to the value of money when prices go up, for example 'Can people buy more or less with £1 now than they could in the past? Does £1 have a lower or higher value now?' As they are completing the sheet, ask them to explain their methods and write a formula for calculating the equivalent value, i.e. value in 1965 x 15 = today's equivalent value. Encourage them not to use calculators, but to use a strategy such as finding x10, halving this to find x5 and adding the two together. During the plenary, discuss that there are other factors which affect the value of goods over time, such as the condition they are in and how rare or desirable they are.

▶ **Value of Money: Level 5**

- **Activity Sheet 16** – Read the credit card statement with the children and explain any unfamiliar vocabulary such as 'credit limit', 'minimum' and 'balance'. Point out the letters 'CR' indicating a credit (money paid in) to the account. Reinforce the difference between a credit card statement, where the balance shows the amount you have to pay, and a bank statement, where the balance shows the amount you possess. Emphasise how important it is for credit card users to make sure they make regular payments.

- **Activity Sheet 17** – Introduce the term 'hire purchase' and explain that it involves paying a deposit (usually a percentage of the shop price) and a number of regular payments. The seller remains the owner of the item until the last payment is made. Talk about the advantages and disadvantages of this method of paying, including the fact that unless the agreement is interest free, the buyer ends up paying more than the shop price. Explain that the longer the period of time the payments are spread over, the more interest is paid. Discuss how to round up prices such as £249.99. During the plenary, compare hire purchase with paying by credit card.

Support

For Activity Sheet 13, the children could find more approximate equivalent values using 1 euro = 60p.

For Activity Sheet 14, change the chart headings to 'How many in £1?', 'How many in £100?' and 'How many in £1000?' Remind the children how to multiply by 100 and 1000 by moving the digits two or three places to the left.

Challenge

After completing Activity Sheet 14, the children could research the price in different countries of basic commodities such as a loaf of bread and a litre of milk. They could look in travel guidebooks and holiday brochures, which often provide this kind of information. Ask them to make a chart of their findings. Explain the phrase 'cost of living' and ask them what they can deduce about the cost of living in the countries they have researched. Ask which countries they think have the highest and the lowest cost of living.

Plenary

Give example figures for buying a large item such as a sofa on hire purchase, for example 'The shop price is £899. The deposit is 10%. You pay £80 per month for 12 months.' Ask the children to calculate the deposit and the total amount paid. Then give figures for paying over 24 months and 36 months, for example £43 per month for 24 months or £32 per month for 36 months. Compare the costs for each of these options.

Display opportunity

Ask the children to write down their views on buying things on credit, giving advantages on one piece of paper and disadvantages on another. Glue them to a display under the headings 'Advantages of having credit' and 'Disadvantages of having credit'.

Extra activities

Copy Generic Sheet 4 (page 31) and cut out the cards. Organise the children into pairs or small groups and give each group a set of cards and a chart showing exchange rates. Check that they understand the dollar symbol. Ask them to take it in turns to pick a card and convert the foreign currency to pounds or vice versa. Emphasise the importance of estimating and rounding skills; explain that an exact answer is not required and they should aim to round the figures so that they can work out an approximation mentally. The others in the group should say whether they think the answer is sensible.

Answers

Activity Sheet 13

1. 6p	2. 12p	3. 30p	4. £1.22
5. £3.05	6. £6.10	7. £12.20	8. £30.50
9. £48.80	10. £73.20	11. £366	
12. £610	13. £5734	14. £12 200	

Activity Sheet 15

1. Cufflinks £30 China plate £165
   Watch £150 Table £225
   Rug £105 Ring £570
   Vase £75 Bookcase £330
2. a) £18 750 b) £1725 c) £36

Activity Sheet 16

1. 4
2. £26.98
3. 6/9/02
4. £374.76
5. £625.24
6. £11
7. £173.68
8. £7.50

Activity Sheet 17

1. a) £25   b) £33   c) £40
2. a) £265 b) £357 c) £442
3. a) £15.01 b) £27.01 c) £42.01

Value of Money – Activity Sheet 13

The euro

One euro is worth 61p. Write the value in pence or pounds of these euro coins and notes.

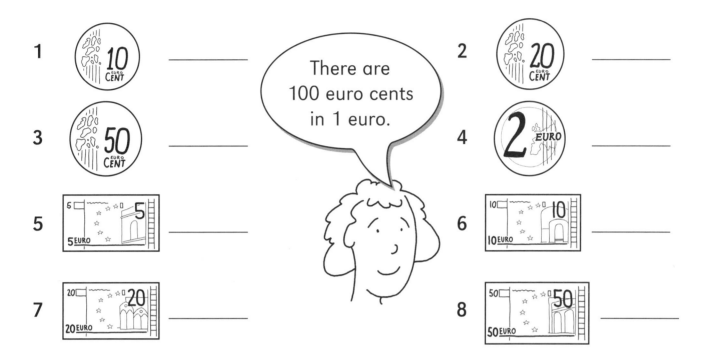

Write the value of these items in pounds.

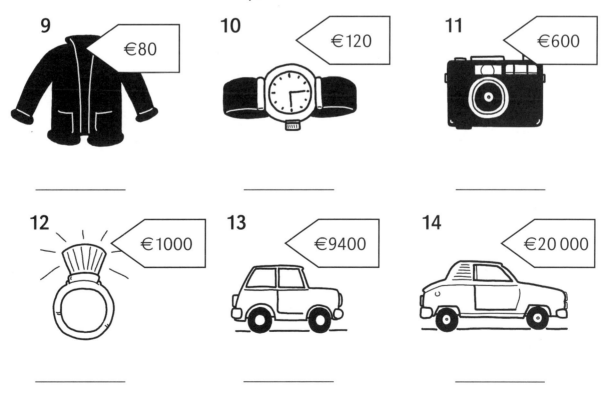

Name_____   ▶ Value of Money – Activity Sheet 14

World currencies

Research exchange rates for currencies around the world, in newspapers or on the Internet.

Fill in this chart.

Unit of currency	How many in £1?	How many in £60?	How many in £5000?
Australian dollar			
Canadian dollar			
Danish kroner			
euro			
Hong Kong dollar			
Israeli shekel			
Japanese yen			
South African rand			
Thai baht			
US dollar			

Which units of currency are closest in value to the pound?
_____

Which units of currency are very different in value from the pound?
_____

PHOTOCOPIABLE
© Hopscotch Educational Publishing 2002

Name_____   ▸ Value of Money – Activity Sheet 15

Past to present

The value of money changes over time. For example, £1 in 1965 is equivalent to about £15 today.

'Equivalent to' means 'worth the same as'.

1   Mr Dunlop bought these things in 1965. Calculate their equivalent price today.

Item	Price paid in 1965	Equivalent price today
Cufflinks	£2	
Watch	£10	
Rug	£7	
Vase	£5	
China plate	£11	
Table	£15	
Ring	£38	
Bookcase	£22	

2   Write today's equivalent value for these amounts of money.

a) In 1965 Mr Dunlop earned £1,250 per year.

Today's equivalent: _____

b) He saved £115 per year.

Today's equivalent: _____

c) He spent £2.40 each week on shopping.

Today's equivalent: _____

PHOTOCOPIABLE
© Hopscotch Educational Publishing 2002

Name_____   ▸ Value of Money – Activity Sheet 16

Credit card statement

Look at Mrs Ward's credit card statement.

Date received by us	Reference no.	Description	Previous balance £173.68
3/9/02	934DNSJE	Perfect Holidays London	£281.50
6/9/02	00PINFLQ	Payment received – thank you	£173.68CR
10/9/02	0MZLA18E	The Bookshop Weymouth	£26.98
11/9/02	S40RWKKB	South West Trains Southampton	£47.80
17/9/02	683GSVRT	Music.co.uk 284-830-921	£18.48
Your credit limit £1000	Minimum payment £11.00	Payment to be credited by 15/10/02	New balance £374.76

Answer the questions.

1 How many purchases has Mrs Ward made this month?
   _____

2 How much did she spend in the bookshop? _____

3 When was the most recent payment received by the credit card company? _____

4 How much has Mrs Ward spent in total this month? _____

5 How much more could she have spent within her credit limit?
   _____

6 What is the minimum amount that Mrs Ward must pay?
   _____

7 What was Mrs Ward's credit card balance last month?
   _____

8 If Mrs Ward does not pay, she will be charged 2% interest. How much is the interest? _____

PHOTOCOPIABLE
© Hopscotch Educational Publishing 2002

Name_____   ▶ Value of Money – Activity Sheet 17

Hire purchase

Hire purchase means that you pay for something monthly instead of all at once.

Look at the chart for buying a mountain bike on hire purchase.

Model	Shop price	Hire purchase over 12 months	
		Deposit	Monthly payment
Blencathra	£249.99	10%	£20
Fairfield	£329.99	10%	£27
Helvellyn	£399.99	10%	£33.50

1 How much is the deposit for each bike if you buy on hire purchase?

  Round the shop price to the nearest pound.

  a) Blencathra _____
  b) Fairfield _____   c) Helvellyn _____

2 Work out how much you pay in total if you buy on hire purchase. Show your workings.

a) Blencathra	b) Fairfield	c) Helvellyn

3 How much more is this than the shop price?

a) Blencathra	b) Fairfield	c) Helvellyn

Name_____   ▸ Value of Money – Generic Sheet 1

Coins and notes

PHOTOCOPIABLE
© Hopscotch Educational Publishing 2002

Name_____   ▸ **Value of Money – Generic Sheet 2**

Accounts sheet cards

20 May You buy a comic for 85p.	29 May You buy some socks for £1.95.	6 June You buy a calculator for £4.99.
23 May You save £3 of your pocket money.	25 May You save £8 of your birthday money.	4 June You buy an ice cream for 80p.
28 May You buy a hairbrush for £2.25.	14 May You save £1.80 of your pocket money.	17 May Your aunt gives you £4.40.
22 May You buy a notebook for 65p.	16 May You buy a ruler for 45p.	31 May You earn £2.50 for washing a car.
19 May You save 90p of your pocket money.	2 June You save £2.05 of your pocket money.	1 June You buy a birthday present for £2.75.

PHOTOCOPIABLE
© Hopscotch Educational Publishing 2002

Name_____   ▶ Value of Money – Generic Sheet 3

Matching values

310p	65p	200p	798p
545p	104p	642p	820p
905p	475p	500p	91p
£5.45	£5.00	£7.98	£0.65
£4.75	£3.10	£9.05	£1.04
£2.00	£8.20	£0.91	£6.42

Currency cards

20 US dollars	35 US dollars	90 US dollars	62 US dollars
1000 US dollars	200 US dollars	2500 US dollars	125 US dollars
30 euros	75 euros	110 euros	59 euros
400 euros	2000 euros	120 euros	165 euros
£4.95 in US dollars	£10.22 in euros	£21.04 in US dollars	£9.56 in euros
£41 in euros	£48.50 in US dollars	£98.12 in euros	£102.30 in US dollars

Calculating: Level 3

UNIT 2: CALCULATING
LEVEL 3

Learning objectives

- To solve problems involving money.
- To find totals and give change.

Key vocabulary

- price, cost, change, total

Resources

- real or plastic coins (or use the coins on Value of Money – Generic Sheet 1, page 28: copy on to stiff card, cut out the coins and glue heads and tails sides back to back)

Introduction

- Revise £.p notation by writing some amounts in pence on the board and asking the children to write them in pounds. Then reverse the activity.

- Show the children an enlarged copy of Generic Sheet 1 (page 58), with prices filled in on the signs at the top of the page, for example 60p and £1.50. First ask questions involving addition and subtraction, for example, 'If you play mini-golf and then go to the cinema, how much does it cost altogether? How much change would you get from £5?' Discuss how to find change by jumping along a blank number line. Ask the children to find possible 'jumps', and encourage all suggestions before pointing out the most efficient method. Then ask them to suggest methods for working out how much it will cost for different numbers of games of mini-golf, or different numbers of children to go to the cinema. Talk about strategies for multiplication and remind them to use known number facts to help them find the answers. Fill in the ready-reckoners on the sheet together.

Activities

- **Activity Sheet 1** – The children should be able to derive the answers to these calculations fairly quickly. Encourage them to use known addition facts and to calculate by counting on. Ask them to check their answers by making each amount of money with coins and seeing that they add up to the correct amount, for example 13p plus 37p makes 50p.

- **Activity Sheet 2** – Remind the children that addition can be done in any order and encourage them to start with the larger number. Ask them how they will check the change from £1 and £5; they should realise that they can add the two amounts together to see that they total £1 or £5.

- **Activity Sheet 3** – Talk about situations in which people have to pay fines and explain the meaning of 'overdue'. These calculations provide practice in the 5 and 10 times tables. As an extension, ask the children to write problems for a partner involving numbers of books being overdue by certain numbers of days.

- **Activity Sheet 4** – Ask the children to work in pairs on this activity. After they have picked a number card, they should replace it and reshuffle the cards regularly. The problems can all be solved by either multiplication or division. Each pair of children will generate a different set of problems; during the plenary ask various children to read out problems for the rest of the class to solve.

- **Activity Sheet 5** – Complete the first ready-reckoner together and explain how the cost of a single item can be worked out by dividing one of the given prices by the appropriate number. For the last ready-reckoner, encourage them to notice the number patterns in adding 99p and ask if they can suggest a quick way of adding 99p (adding £1, then subtracting 1p). Discuss the fact that many prices end in 99p so it is useful to be able to add 99p mentally.

- **Activity Sheet 6** – Introduce the activity by reading out a money problem of this type and demonstrating how to decide which number operation to use. Then model how to explain

▶ Calculating: Level 3

how the problem was solved and write a number sentence for the problem. Encourage the children to write number sentences for the problems on the backs of the cards, as well as explaining their methods orally.

🕓 Support

Copy Generic Sheet 1 (page 58) and fill in prices on the signs according to the children's level of attainment, for example 20p and £3. Ask them to fill in the ready-reckoners, taking care to put the decimal point in the correct place. Encourage them to notice that once they have completed the calculations up to 10 times the price, they can use these answers to help them with the remaining calculations, for example the cost of 13 games is the cost of 10 games plus the cost of 3 games.

🕓 Challenge

To provide practice in multiplying by 6, 7, 8 or 9, change the amounts of the fines on Activity Sheet 3. For example, fines on books could be 6p, 7p, 8p or 9p per day. Fines on cassettes could be 30p per day to give more challenging calculations.

When the children have completed Activity Sheet 5, set them calculations to answer using their completed ready-reckoners, for example 'What is the cost of 15 pens?', 'What is the cost of 16 bags?' and 'What is the cost of 19 mugs?'

Copy Generic Sheet 2 (page 59) and fill in entrance prices according to the children's level of attainment, for example 'Adult £8, Child £4.50, Student £6.20'. Ask them to fill in the ready-reckoners and then answer the questions at the bottom, which involve extracting the relevant information from the ready-reckoners and calculating the total.

🕓 Plenary

Show the children some completed ready-reckoners which include several mistakes. Ask the children to find the mistakes and say how many they think there are. Then invite some children to come to the front and correct the errors, explaining how they could recognise them.

🕓 Display opportunity

Provide catalogues and ask the children to each choose an item, cut it out and create a ready-reckoner from one to ten. Display the pictures and ready-reckoners and use them to generate calculations for the class to answer, involving finding totals or finding the difference between prices.

🕓 Extra activities

Copy Generic Sheet 3 (page 60) on to card. Organise the children into groups of three or four and ask them to cut out the spinners and push a pencil through the centre of each. They should take turns to spin one spinner, then the other, and find the total of the two amounts of money. The others in the group should check that the answer is correct. Encourage them to use efficient calculating methods such as doubling and multiplying as well as adding. They could win a sum of money such as 50p for each correct answer; the winner is the player with the most money when each child has had five turns.

🕓 Answers

Activity Sheet 1

1. a) 6p   b) 25p   c) 11p
   d) 37p   e) 43p   f) 28p
2. a) 35p   b) 15p   c) 55p
   d) 95p   e) 75p   f) 85p
   g) 23p   h) 49p   i) 64p
3. a) £2.50 b) £1.10
   c) £0.40 d) £3.50

Activity Sheet 2

1.   2.
a) Correct   a) Correct   i) Correct
b) Incorrect (24p)   b) Incorrect (45p)   j) Correct
c) Incorrect (41p)   c) Incorrect (18p)   k) Incorrect
d) Correct   d) Correct   (£4.70)
e) Incorrect (94p)   e) Correct   l) Incorrect
f) Correct   f) Incorrect (92p)   (£1.50)
g) Correct   g) Incorrect (£2.90)
h) Incorrect (£1.12)   h) Correct

Activity Sheet 3

1. a) 15p   b) 40p   c) 25p
   d) 45p   e) 60p   f) 75p
2. a) £1   b) 60p   c) £1.40
   d) £1   e) £1.80   f) 60p

Activity Sheet 6

Amanda: 5p
Jonathan: 5 weeks
Mohammed: 11 weeks
Louise: 28p
Alan's sister: £1.20
Mr Hill: £1.60
Melanie's sister: £13.50
Mrs Clegg's children: £1.50
Jack: 51p
Nita: 60p

Name_____ ▸ Calculating – Activity Sheet 1

Money spiders

1 Make the pairs of spiders total 50p. Write the missing numbers.

a) 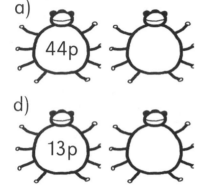　b) 　c)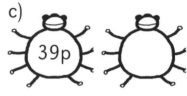

d) 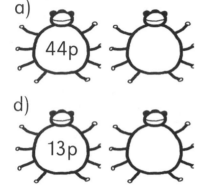　e) 　f)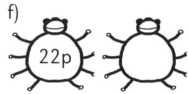

2 Make these pairs of spiders total £1.

a) 　b) 　c)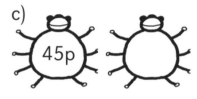

d) 　e) 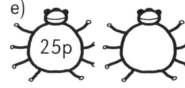　f)

g) 　h) 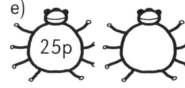　i)

3 Make these pairs of spiders total £5.

a)  　b)

c) 　d)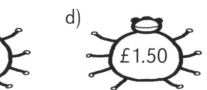

PHOTOCOPIABLE
© Hopscotch Educational Publishing 2002

Name_____ ▸ Calculating – Activity Sheet 2

Be a teacher!

This is Molly's maths homework. Mark her calculations.
Correct the wrong answers.

1
a) 43p + 8p = 51p

b) 12p + 9p + 3p = 23p

c) 11p + 21p + 9p = 40p

d) 27p + 35p = 62p

e) 68p + 26p = 84p

f) 40p + 64p = £1.04

g) 90p + 90p = £1.80

h) 82p + 30p = £1.22

2

	Cost	Change from £1		Cost	Change from £5
a)	25p	75p	g)	£2.10	£3.90
b)	55p	35p	h)	£4.40	£0.60
c)	82p	28p	i)	£3.80	£1.20
d)	94p	6p	j)	£2.60	£2.40
e)	31p	69p	k)	£0.30	£4.80
f)	8p	94p	l)	£3.50	£2.50

Name_____   ▸ Calculating – Activity Sheet 3

Library fines

1 Library fines are 5p per book per day. Calculate the fines on these books.

a) 3 days overdue   Fine: _____

b) 8 days overdue   Fine: _____

c) 5 days overdue   Fine: _____

d) 9 days overdue   Fine: _____

e) 12 days overdue   Fine: _____

f) 15 days overdue   Fine: _____

2 Library fines on video cassettes are 10p per cassette per day. Calculate the fines.

a) 1 cassette 10 days overdue.   Fine: _____

b) 1 cassette 6 days overdue.   Fine: _____

c) 1 cassette 14 days overdue.   Fine: _____

d) 2 cassettes 5 days overdue.   Fine: _____

e) 2 cassettes 9 days overdue.   Fine: _____

f) 3 cassettes 2 days overdue.   Fine: _____

PHOTOCOPIABLE
© Hopscotch Educational Publishing 2002

Name_____   ▸ Calculating – Activity Sheet 4

Create a problem!

Cut out the number cards below. Place them face down.

Read the problems. Pick a number card for each question and write the number in the box. Replace the number card. Work out the answer.

1 Ian buys ☐ lollipops at 12p each. How much does he pay?
   Answer: _____

2 A bus trip costs 30p. How much does it cost for ☐ children?
   Answer: _____

3 ☐ children share 60p. How much do they each receive?
   Answer: _____

4 John saves 80p a week for ☐ weeks. How much does he save?
   Answer: _____

5 Becky buys ☐ greetings cards at 70p each. How much does she pay? Answer: _____

6 ☐ children share £30. How much do they each receive?
   Answer: _____

7 Helen has ☐ rides at the fairground. Each ride costs £1.20. How much does she pay? Answer: _____

8 ☐ children share £1.20. How much do they each receive?
   Answer: _____

| 2 | 3 | 4 | 5 | 10 |

PHOTOCOPIABLE
© Hopscotch Educational Publishing 2002

Name_____   ▸ Calculating – Activity Sheet 5

Reckoning day

A ready-reckoner helps you to work out the cost of several items which are all the same price.

Complete this ready-reckoner.

pen 30p

2 pens	3 pens	4 pens	5 pens	6 pens	7 pens	8 pens	9 pens	10 pens
60p	90p	£1.20			£2.10			

Fill in these ready-reckoners. Write the prices on the tags.

dice _____

2 dice	3 dice	4 dice	5 dice	6 dice	7 dice	8 dice	9 dice	10 dice
50p		£1.00			£1.75			

hat _____

2 hats	3 hats	4 hats	5 hats	6 hats	7 hats	8 hats	9 hats	10 hats
			£40			£64		

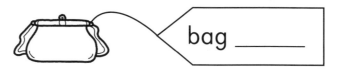
bag _____

2 bags	3 bags	4 bags	5 bags	6 bags	7 bags	8 bags	9 bags	10 bags
	£7.50	£10.00						

mug _____

2 mugs	3 mugs	4 mugs	5 mugs	6 mugs	7 mugs	8 mugs	9 mugs	10 mugs
£1.98				£5.94				£9.90

PHOTOCOPIABLE

Name_____   ▶ Calculating – Activity Sheet 6

Problem cards

Cut out the cards. Take turns with a partner to pick one.

Find the answer and explain to your partner how you worked it out.

Amanda has six 20p coins and a 10p coin. She spends £1.25. How much does she have left?	Jonathan saves £1.20 a week. How long will it take him to save £6.00?
Mohammed is saving up for a game which costs £5.50. He saves 50p a week. How long will it take him?	Louise buys two drinks at 36p each. What is her change from £1?
Alan gets £1.80 a week pocket money. His younger sister gets two-thirds as much. What does she get?	Mr Hill went out with £10. He spent £2.30, £4.50 and £1.60. How much did he have left?
Melanie's sister earns £4.50 per hour. How much does she earn in 3 hours?	Mrs Clegg shares £6 between her four children. How much do they each receive?
Jack buys a sandwich for 90p, a drink for 32p and an apple for 27p. What is his change from £2?	Nita saved £4.80. It took her 8 weeks. How much did she save each week?

PHOTOCOPIABLE
© Hopscotch Educational Publishing 2002

▶ Calculating: Level 4

▶ UNIT 2: CALCULATING
LEVEL 4

🕒 Learning objectives

- To use all four operations to solve word problems involving money.
- To find simple percentages.

Key vocabulary

- cost, change, total, discount, fraction, percentage, %

🕒 Resources

- calculators

🕒 Introduction

- Discuss the use of calculators and explain that a calculator is sometimes the most efficient way to calculate or to check an answer but that it should never be used as a replacement for mental or written methods. Demonstrate that a calculator display can be misleading when used to solve money problems, for example 4.7 on the display must not be recorded as £4.7 but £4.70. Emphasise the importance of using the same unit when adding or subtracting amounts of money by showing what happens when £23 is inputted instead of 23p. Give the children calculations to try out using calculators. Encourage them always to check that the answer is sensible.

- Discuss percentage as the number of parts in every hundred and revise the % sign. Reinforce that 25% equals a quarter, 50% equals a half and 75% equals three-quarters. Explain that finding 10% is the same as dividing by 10, i.e. moving the digits one place to the right. Introduce the word 'discount' and let the children practise finding a 10% discount on various amounts.

🕒 Activities

- **Activity Sheet 7** – Encourage the children to do the calculations mentally if possible, or by making jottings. Discuss strategies for adding three amounts of money, such as adding two amounts and then the third, or totalling all the pence and then all the pounds. Point out that when two amounts have units digits which total ten, it is a good idea to total these amounts first. As an extension, draw some 'rectangle totals' on the board (with four amounts to total instead of three) for the children to solve.

- **Activity Sheet 8** – The children could be allowed to use calculators for this activity, but ask them to calculate mentally wherever possible. Remind them that a quick way to add amounts ending in 99p is to round the amount up to the next pound and then subtract 1p from the total. Encourage them to find the change by counting on from the total to £20.

- **Activity Sheet 9** – This activity offers practice in doubling amounts of money. Revise strategies for doubling, such as doubling the tens first and then the units. Encourage the children to calculate the doubles mentally and to record their workings for the additions in the spaces provided.

- **Activity Sheet 10** – Help the children to find quick ways of calculating, for example 18 x 5p has the same answer as 9 x 10p. To multiply by 9p, they can multiply by 10p and then subtract 1p per length. As an extension activity, they could make a ready-reckoner for each child, for amounts between 2p and 20p per length.

- **Activity Sheet 11** – This activity involves dividing a whole number of pounds by 2, 4, 5 or 10 to give pounds and pence. Discuss possible calculation strategies with the children, such as sharing out the tens first and then the units, or rounding to the nearest ten and then adjusting. They could check their answers using a calculator or using the inverse operation, i.e. multiplication.

- **Activity Sheet 12** – Revise strategies for calculating percentages, for example calculating 20% by finding 10% and then doubling; calculating 5% by finding 10% and

▶ Calculating: Level 4

then halving; and calculating 75% by finding 25% and then multiplying by three. The children could check each other's answers using a calculator. If they give an incorrect answer they should put the cards back.

- **Activity Sheet 13** – Revise the word 'fraction' and simple fractions such as a quarter, a third and a fifth. Reinforce the links between fractions and division, for example dividing by four to find a quarter and dividing by three to find a third.

- **Activity Sheet 14** – Discuss how to find 10% by dividing by 10 (moving the digits one place to the right). Remind the children that a discount is 'money off', so they should subtract the discount to find the final total. Explain the @ sign and revise rounding to two decimal places.

Support

Before beginning Activity Sheet 12, discuss percentages and write hints on the board to help the children, for example '25% = a quarter. Halve and halve again to find a quarter.' They could work together playing a simple matching game using some or all of the cards.

Use Generic Sheet 4 (page 61) for matching activities which give practice in mental multiplication and division. Ask the children to sort the cards into pairs which have the same answer.

Challenge

To test the children's rapid recall of percentages, give them the question cards only from Activity Sheet 12. Ask them to put the cards in a line in order of value of the answers, without writing down the answers. This could be done in a group or they can work individually and then compare and discuss their order with a friend.

Plenary

Provide lists of amounts to total, with four amounts in each list. Give some which can be easily totalled mentally and some for which calculators may be needed. Point out the need for the children to ask themselves 'Can I do this mentally?' before they tackle any calculation. Ask them to decide how they will total the amounts, then work out the answers together.

Display opportunity

Draw two large circles on a display and label them 'Calculator' and 'No calculator'. Using the lists of amounts from the plenary, sort the calculations into the correct circles on the display. Discuss the reasons for the children's choices.

Extra activities

Copy the bingo cards on Generic Sheet 5 (page 62) on to card. Give the children one each and ask them to fill in the empty squares with any multiples of 10p less than £10. Play 'doubles bingo', for example call out 'double 80p' or 'double £2.35'. (Call out any multiples of 5p less than £5.) Children who have the answer on their card cross it out. The first to cross out all their squares is the winner.

Answers

Activity Sheet 7

1. £8.43   2. £1.08   3. £9.11   4. £10.77   5. £21.64
6. 36p   7. £0.40   8. £0.27   9. £3.63   10. £2.25

Activity Sheet 8

1. Cost: £11.49   Change: £8.51
2. Cost: £16.87   Change: £3.13
3. Cost: £14.97   Change: £5.03
4. Cost: £17.10   Change: £2.90
5. Cost: £14.63   Change: £5.37
6. Cost: £13.91   Change: £6.09
7. Cost: £17.06   Change: £2.94
8. Cost: £18.60   Change: £1.40

Activity Sheet 9

Monday: £15.16   Tuesday: £30.50   Wednesday: £8.86
Thursday: £5.16   Friday: £7.46

Activity Sheet 10

1. a) 90p   b) £1.15   c) £1.30
   d) 85p   e) £1.75   f) £1.60
2. a) £1.62   b) £2.07   c) £2.34
   d) £1.53   e) £3.15   f) £2.88
3. £4.60   4. 30p   5. 40p   6. £39   7. £1.20

Activity Sheet 11

1. £29.50   2. £54   3. £51.40   4. £66.40
5. £22.75   6. £85.50   7. £103.70   8. £120.40

Activity Sheet 13

1. a) £3   b) £4   c) £5
2. a) £4   b) £2.50   c) £1.75
3. a) £15   b) 3/5

Activity Sheet 14

1. £7.35   £0.74   £6.61
2. £10.71   £1.07   £9.64
3. £13.38   £1.34   £12.04
4. £21.19   £2.12   £19.07
5. £32.86   £3.29   £29.57

Triangle totals

Total the amounts in each triangle. Write the answer in the centre.

Look out for units digits that total 10.

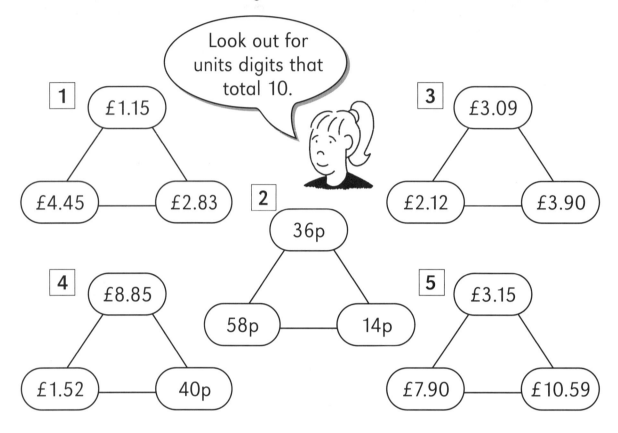

The total is in the centre. Write the missing value.

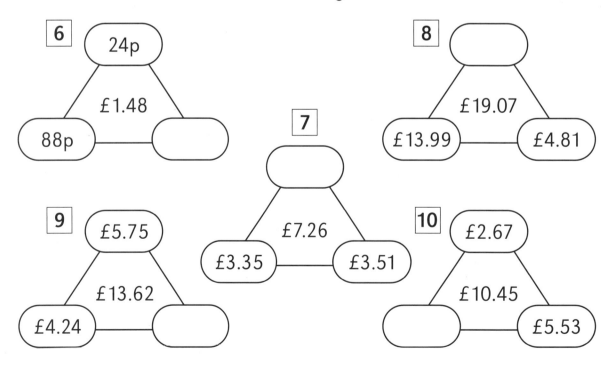

Name_____   ▸ Calculating – Activity Sheet 8

Gift shopping

Work out the cost of each purchase and the change from £20.

1 A calculator at £8.99 and some batteries at £2.50.

   Cost: _____   Change from £20: _____

2 A vase at £11.65 and some flowers at £5.22.

   Cost: _____   Change from £20: _____

3 Three boxes of chocolates at £4.99 each.

   Cost: _____   Change from £20: _____

4 Two candlesticks at £7.35 each and two candles at £1.20 each.

   Cost: _____   Change from £20: _____

5 A CD at £12.50, some giftwrap at 85p and a card at £1.28.

   Cost: _____   Change from £20: _____

6 A lamp at £12.15 and two light bulbs at 88p each.

   Cost: _____   Change from £20: _____

7 A scarf at £7.85, a hat at £5.49 and some gloves at £3.72.

   Cost: _____   Change from £20: _____

8 Four mugs at £4.65 each.

   Cost: _____   Change from £20: _____

PHOTOCOPIABLE
© Hopscotch Educational Publishing 2002

Name_____   ▸ Calculating – Activity Sheet 9

Double trouble

Susie and Sarah are twins. They always do exactly the same as each other and buy the same things. Read Susie's holiday diary.

Monday
Went swimming for £1.95. Bought a book for £5.63.

Tuesday
Paid £11.80 to go to the theme park. Spent £3.45 on food.

Wednesday
Spent £2.56 in the chemist's and £1.87 in the newsagent's.

Thursday
Went to the seaside. Bought a hot dog for £1.42 and a drink for 37p. Later bought an ice cream for 79p.

Friday
Went to the cinema. Paid £2.68 for the ticket. Bought a drink for £1.05.

Work out how much both girls spent each day.

Double the amounts!

Monday	Tuesday	Wednesday	Thursday	Friday

PHOTOCOPIABLE
© Hopscotch Educational Publishing 2002

Name_____   ▸ Calculating – Activity Sheet 10

Sponsored swim

Class 4L did a sponsored swim for charity. The chart shows how many lengths these children swam.

Name	Kath	Neil	Sara	Matthew	Nagmi	Daniel
No. of lengths:	18	23	26	17	35	32

1 Mr Sykes sponsored the children 5p per length. How much did he pay each child?

   a) Kath _____   b) Neil _____   c) Sara _____

   d) Matthew _____   e) Nagmi _____   f) Daniel _____

2 Mrs McCann sponsored the children 9p per length. How much did she pay each child?

   a) Kath _____   b) Neil _____   c) Sara _____

   d) Matthew _____   e) Nagmi _____   f) Daniel _____

3 Neil's sister sponsored him 20p per length. How much did she pay him?
   _____

4 Kath's dad paid her £5.40. How much did he sponsor her per length?
   _____

5 Matthew's mum paid him £6.80. How much did she sponsor him per length? _____

6 Sara was sponsored a total of £1.50 per length. How much did she collect? _____

7 Nagmi collected £42.00 in total. How much was this per length?
   _____

Name_____   ▸ Calculating – Activity Sheet 11

Prize winners

These people went on television game shows in teams. Work out how much each person receives when the prize money is shared out.

1 James and Ruth
   Total prize money: £59
   Each person receives: _____

2 The Banks family
   Total prize money: £216
   Each person receives: _____

3 The Grange Manor School team
   Total prize money: £514
   Each person receives: _____

4 The Davies family
   Total prize money: £332
   Each person receives: _____

5 The Carpenter family
   Total prize money: £91
   Each person receives: _____

6 Jennifer and Wendy
   Total prize money: £171
   Each person receives: _____

7 The West End School team
   Total prize money: £1037
   Each person receives: _____

8 The Ahmed family
   Total prize money: £602
   Each person receives: _____

PHOTOCOPIABLE
© Hopscotch Educational Publishing 2002

Name_____   ▸ Calculating – Activity Sheet 12

Percentage cards

Cut out the cards and spread them out. With a partner, take turns to pick a question card.

Find the card that shows the answer.

If you are correct, keep the cards. Who collects the most?

What is 25% of £10?	£5.50	What is 30% of £5?	50p
£2.00	What is 10% of £14?	£4.00	What is 75% of £1?
What is 90% of £1?	£1.00	What is 25% of £12?	£6.00
80p	What is 60% of £2?	60p	What is 50% of £7?
What is 20% of £5?	90p	What is 75% of £8?	£3.00
£1.20	What is 20% of £4?	£3.50	What is 10% of £6?
What is 25% of £2?	£2.50	What is 50% of £11?	£1.50
£1.40	What is 5% of £40?	75p	What is 80% of £5?

47

PHOTOCOPIABLE
© Hopscotch Educational Publishing 2002

Birthday money

Three children had their birthdays last month. Solve their fraction problems.

1 Carol received £12 birthday money.

   a) She spent a quarter of it on jelly beans. How much were the jelly beans? _____

   b) She spent a third of it on a game. How much was the game? _____

   c) She saved the rest. How much did she save? _____

2 Adrian received £10 birthday money.

   a) He spent two-fifths of it on a pen. How much was the pen? _____

   b) He spent a quarter of it on a model kit. How much was the kit? _____

   c) He spent half of the remainder on football stickers. How much were the stickers?

   _____

3 Martin received a fifth of his birthday money from his uncle. His uncle gave him £3.

   a) How much birthday money did Martin receive in total? _____

   b) His aunt gave him £9. What fraction of his birthday money did she give him?

   _____

Name_____   ▸ Calculating – Activity Sheet 14

Pete's Pizzas

At Pete's Pizzas, customers get a 10% discount if they collect their pizzas. Fill in the pizza bills.

1
1 pizza @	£2.95
1 pizza @	£3.22
1 bread @	£1.18
Total	_____
10% discount	_____
Final total	_____

Round the discount to the nearest penny. Remember that 0.5 rounds up.

2
1 pizza @	£3.90
1 pizza @	£4.43
1 bread @	£1.18
2 drinks @	£0.60 each
Total	_____
10% discount	_____
Final total	_____

3
2 pizzas @	£3.90 each
1 pizza @	£3.22
2 breads @	£1.18 each
Total	_____
10% discount	_____
Final total	_____

4
3 pizzas @	£2.95 each
2 pizzas @	£3.22 each
5 drinks @	£1.18 each
Total	_____
10% discount	_____
Final total	_____

5
4 pizzas @	£4.43 each
3 breads @	£1.18 each
4 desserts @	£2.90 each
Total	_____
10% discount	_____
Final total	_____

PHOTOCOPIABLE
© Hopscotch Educational Publishing 2002

Calculating: Level 5

UNIT 2: CALCULATING
LEVEL 5

Learning objectives

- To solve word problems involving money.
- To calculate percentages such as VAT.

Key vocabulary

- total, discount, profit, loss, fraction, percentage, %, currency

Resources

- calculators

Introduction

- Ask the children where they have seen percentages relating to money and make a list of their suggestions. Talk about VAT, discounts in shops and service charges on food bills. Write an example food bill on the board and calculate a service charge of 10% together. Model how to record the workings. Then do the same for a 20% charge, by finding 10% and doubling.

- Introduce the vocabulary 'profit' and 'loss' and explain that these are often calculated in percentages. Give examples of profit based on a shopkeeper, for example 'Mrs Dunn runs a small shop. She buys goods from a wholesaler and makes a 10% profit on everything she sells.' Give examples of prices in the shop, for example 'Mrs Dunn buys crisps for 20p a bag. How much does she sell them for?' (22p). Repeat for other items and prices. Explain loss in a similar way, for example in the context of buying and selling cars.

Activities

- **Activity Sheet 15** – Reinforce the links between fractions and division, for example dividing by four to find a quarter and dividing by three to find a third. Remind the children how to find 10% of an amount of money by dividing by 10, and show how this can be used to find 20%, 30%, 40% and so on.

- **Activity Sheet 16** – Emphasise that profit is equivalent to 'plus' (or increase in value) and loss is equivalent to 'minus' (or decrease in value). Revise finding percentages and encourage the children to find 20%, 40% and 80% by finding 10% and doubling once, twice or three times. As an extension, they could find the new value of each item by adding the profit or subtracting the loss.

- **Activity Sheet 17** – Discuss VAT and explain that the rate is 17.5%. Ask the children if they have ever seen VAT added on to a bill and explain that it is already included in many prices. Demonstrate the method of finding 17.5% explained on the activity sheet, using a simple amount such as £400. Ask the children to record their workings on the back of the sheet. When they have finished, ask them to check their answers by finding 1% mentally (dividing by 100) and multiplying this by 17.5 on a calculator.

- **Activity Sheet 18** – This activity provides practice in calculating 10%, 20% and 40% of large amounts. Explain to the children that house values often increase at a greater rate than inflation and that houses in different areas increase at different rates. Check that they understand that they need to add the percentage on to the old value in order to find the new value.

- **Activity Sheet 19** – This activity involves multiplying and dividing amounts of money by two-digit numbers. Revise written methods for these types of calculations and encourage the children to choose the method they find easiest. Ask them to record their workings on the back of the sheet.

- **Activity Sheet 20** – The children will need to look in newspapers or on the Internet to find out exchange rates. (An online currency converter can be found at www.xe.com/ucc/.) Encourage them to round the exchange rates as necessary to make the numbers easier to work with.

▶ Calculating: Level 5

🕒 Support

Give the children copies of Generic Sheet 6 (page 63). Ask them to cut out the cards and find a number sentence to match the calculation in each word problem. Point out that there are more number sentences than word problems. When they have done this, ask them to solve the word problems using calculators or written methods and write the answers on the backs of the cards.

🕒 Challenge

When the children have completed Activity Sheet 17, write some amounts on the board at random. Ask them to work out the VAT on the amounts quickly, using a calculator. They should round their answers to the nearest penny.

Use the cards from Generic Sheet 6 (page 63). Initially, give the children the word problem cards only. Ask them to write a number sentence to match each problem. When they have done this, give them the number sentence cards to check against what they have written. Ask them to solve the word problems using calculators or written methods. As an extension, they could make up word problems for the spare number sentence cards.

🕒 Plenary

Consolidate finding percentages and fractions of amounts of money by organising the children into groups and having a quiz. Ask questions such as 'What is two-fifths of £15?' and 'What is 80% of £80?' Each group should decide on the answer together and write it down. A point is scored for every correct answer.

🕒 Display opportunity

Display a map of the world with a chart of exchange rates alongside. Tell the class they are going on a world trip; each week they visit a new country on the map and create a currency ready-reckoner for the country. The ready-reckoner on Activity Sheet 20 could be used as a template.

🕒 Extra activities

Use Generic Sheet 7 (page 64) to give practice in finding the total of two, three or four amounts of money. Ask the children to pick cards at random and total them. To practise subtracting, they can pick two cards and find the difference.

🕒 Answers

Activity Sheet 15

1. £51
2. £53
3. 20p
4. a) £112.20
   b) £33.66
5. a) £97.65
   b) £39.06

Activity Sheet 16

1. £40 profit   2. £23 loss
3. £130 loss   4. £33 profit
5. £245 profit   6. £152 loss
7. £500 profit   8. £26 loss
9. £292 loss   10. £656 profit

Activity Sheet 17

1. VAT: £35   2. VAT: £87.50
   Total: £235   Total: £587.50

3. VAT: £38.50   4. VAT: £70.35
   Total: £258.50   Total: £472.35

5. VAT: £13.65   6. VAT: £27.30
   Total: £91.65   Total: £183.30

Activity Sheet 18

1. Rise: £8600
   New value: £94 600
2. Rise: £13 400
   New value: £147 400
3. Rise: £9550
   New value: £105 050
4. Rise: £32 000
   New value: £192 000
5. Rise: £12 400
   New value: £74 400
6. Rise: £21 600
   New value: £129 600
7. Rise: £36 000
   New value: £126 000
8. Rise: £58 000
   New value: £203 000
9. Rise: £45 200
   New value: £158 200

Activity Sheet 19

1. a) £10.50
   b) £8.40
   c) £6.30
2. a) £3.50
   b) £2.80
   c) £2.10
3. a) £39
   b) £48.75
   c) £65

Summer Fair

The Mount School had a Summer Fair. Can you solve their money problems?

1. The Lucky Dip made £76.50. The tombola made two-thirds that amount. How much did the tombola make? _____

2. The Name-the-Teddy game made £66.25. Last year it made four-fifths that amount. How much did it make last year?

_____

3. Class 6J ran the raffle. They made a total of £78. They sold 390 tickets. What was the price per ticket? _____

4. Class 6R ran the drinks stall. They sold 340 drinks at 33p each.
   a) How much money did they take?

   _____

   b) Their profit was 30% of the total. How much profit did they make?

   _____

5. Class 6C ran the food stall. They sold 225 bags of crisps at 21p each and 180 bags of sweets at 28p each.
   a) How much money did they take?

   _____

   b) Their profit was 40% of the total. How much profit did they make? _____

Profit and loss

When an item increases in value, you make a profit.

When an item decreases in value, you make a loss.

Write how much profit or loss is made on these items. One has been done for you.

1 was £400 increased by 10%

£40 profit

2 was £230 decreased by 10%

_____

3 was £650 decreased by 20%

_____

4 was £110 increased by 30%

_____

5 was £490 increased by 50%

_____

6 was £380 decreased by 40%

_____

7 was £1250 increased by 40%

_____

8 was £520 decreased by 5%

_____

9 was £1460 decreased by 20%

_____

10  was £820 increased by 80%

_____

Name_____   ▸ Calculating – Activity Sheet 17

House repairs

The Owen family are moving house. They have asked some people to do repairs on the house.

Read the bills. Work out the VAT and the total.

To find 17.5%, first find 10%.
Then halve this to find 5%.
Then halve this to find 2.5%.
Add 10%, 5% and 2.5% to make 17.5%.

1 Electrician's bill
Parts and labour   £200.00
VAT @ 17.5%   _____
Total   _____

2 Builder's bill
Parts and labour   £500.00
VAT @ 17.5%   _____
Total   _____

3 Joiner's bill
Parts and labour   £220.00
VAT @ 17.5%   _____
Total   _____

4 Decorator's bill
Parts and labour   £402.00
VAT @ 17.5%   _____
Total   _____

5 Plumber's bill
Parts and labour   £78.00
VAT @ 17.5%   _____
Total   _____

6 Roofer's bill
Parts and labour   £156.00
VAT @ 17.5%   _____
Total   _____

PHOTOCOPIABLE
© Hopscotch Educational Publishing 2002

Name_____   ▸ Calculating – Activity Sheet 18

Rising values

House values in Lockwood have risen by 10%. Calculate the new value of each house.

1 Old value £86 000

10% rise _____

New value _____

2 Old value £134 000

10% rise _____

New value _____

3 Old value £95 500

10% rise _____

New value _____

House values in Moortown have risen by 20%. Calculate the new value of each house.

4 Old value £160 000

20% rise _____

New value _____

5 Old value £62 000

20% rise _____

New value _____

6 Old value £108 000

20% rise _____

New value _____

House values in Netherton have risen by 40%. Calculate the new value of each house.

7 Old value £90 000

40% rise _____

New value _____

8 Old value £145 000

40% rise _____

New value _____

9 Old value £113 000

40% rise _____

New value _____

PHOTOCOPIABLE
© Hopscotch Educational Publishing 2002

Name_____ ▸ Calculating – Activity Sheet 19

A group outing

Mr Russell is planning an outing for a group of children. Help him to work out the costs.

1 It will cost £126 to hire a minibus.

   What will be the cost per child if there are:

   a) 12 children in the group? _____

   b) 15 children in the group? _____

   c) 20 children in the group? _____

2 The petrol for the trip will cost £42.

   What will be the cost per child if there are:

   a) 12 children in the group? _____

   b) 15 children in the group? _____

   c) 20 children in the group? _____

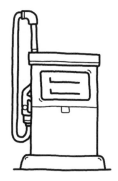

3 The museum entrance charge is £3.25 per child.

   What will be the total entrance charge if there are:

   a) 12 children in the group? _____

   b) 15 children in the group? _____

   c) 20 children in the group? _____

PHOTOCOPIABLE
© Hopscotch Educational Publishing 2002

Name _____   ▸ Calculating – Activity Sheet 20

Currency converter

Choose a currency and find out the exchange rate.
Fill in the ready-reckoner.

Currency: _____

Exchange rate: £1 = _____

Amount in £	Amount in _____	Amount in £	Amount in _____
1		20	
2		30	
3		40	
4		50	
5		60	
6		70	
8		90	
9		100	
10		500	

Use the ready-reckoner to help you convert these amounts.

£13   £29   £57

_____   _____   _____

£166   £85   £601

_____   _____   _____

£350   £10 000   £973

_____   _____   _____

PHOTOCOPIABLE
© Hopscotch Educational Publishing 2002

Name_____   ▶ Calculating – Generic Sheet 1

Ready-reckoners

Mini-golf	Cinema
_____ per game	_____ per person

1 game = _____   1 person = _____
2 games = _____   2 people = _____
3 games = _____   3 people = _____
4 games = _____   4 people = _____
5 games = _____   5 people = _____
6 games = _____   6 people = _____
7 games = _____   7 people = _____
8 games = _____   8 people = _____
9 games = _____   9 people = _____
10 games = _____   10 people = _____
11 games = _____   11 people = _____
12 games = _____   12 people = _____
13 games = _____   13 people = _____
14 games = _____   14 people = _____
15 games = _____   15 people = _____
16 games = _____   16 people = _____
17 games = _____   17 people = _____
18 games = _____   18 people = _____
19 games = _____   19 people = _____
20 games = _____   20 people = _____

Name_____   ▸ Calculating – Generic Sheet 2

Theme park reckoner

 **Dinoland**

Entrance prices

Adult _____   Child _____   Student _____

1 adult = _____	1 child = _____	1 student = _____
2 adults = _____	2 children = _____	2 students = _____
3 adults = _____	3 children = _____	3 students = _____
4 adults = _____	4 children = _____	4 students = _____
5 adults = _____	5 children = _____	5 students = _____
6 adults = _____	6 children = _____	6 students = _____
7 adults = _____	7 children = _____	7 students = _____
8 adults = _____	8 children = _____	8 students = _____
9 adults = _____	9 children = _____	9 students = _____
10 adults = _____	10 children = _____	10 students = _____

1 adult and 2 children = _____   3 adults and 3 students = _____

2 adults and 2 students = _____   8 adults and 10 children = _____

2 adults and 1 child = _____   3 adults and 6 students = _____

4 adults and 5 children = _____   5 adults and 9 children = _____

3 adults, 2 children and 1 student = _____

4 adults, 6 children and 2 students = _____

Spinners

▶ Calculating – Generic Sheet 3

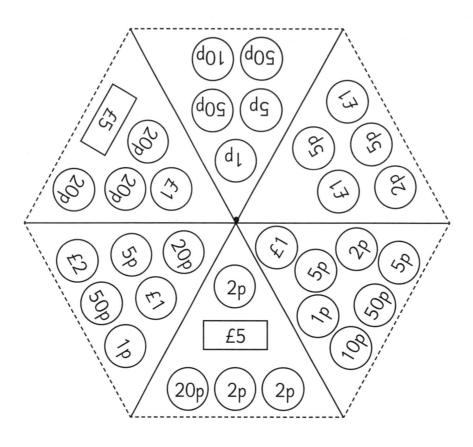

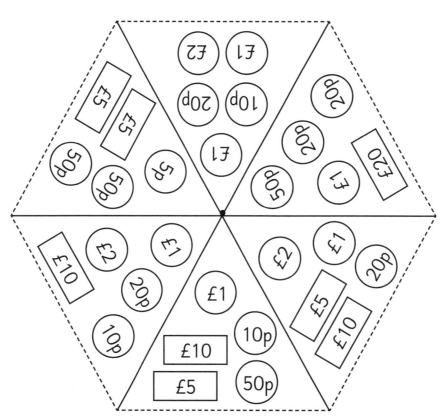

Matching pairs

3 x 20p	£6.40 ÷ 8	12p x 6	35p x 4
7p x 5	£2.88 ÷ 4	12 x 5p	£1.40 ÷ 4
£10 ÷ 8	£20 ÷ 20	25p x 5	20 x 2p
£1.20 ÷ 3	£4 ÷ 5	£4.20 ÷ 6	9 x 15p
75p x 2	£2.70 ÷ 2	£2.70 ÷ 3	20 x 5p
18 x 5p	£4.90 ÷ 7	28p x 5	£6 ÷ 4

Doubles bingo cards

£7.00		£5.90
£3.60	£2.20	
		70p

	£3.20	50p
£4.30		
	£5.80	£8.80

	£2.70	40p
	£1.40	
£9.00		£6.10

£1.50		£9.10
	£6.40	
£4.00	£2.80	

£1.60	£4.30	
£6.70	£9.00	
	£5.20	

£8.30		
£7.30	£3.40	£5.00
		90p

Number stories

Naomi bought six pencils at 18p and two pens at 34p. How much did she pay altogether?	Richard changed £20 into euros. There are 1.63 euros to £1. How many euros did he get?
160 people bought hamburgers. They paid £240 in total. What was the cost of each hamburger?	Tamsin bought a CD. Her change from £20 was £8.51. What did the CD cost?
Tariq saved £1.80 each week. How much did he save in one year?	Saira gave £2 a month to charity. How much did she give in three years?
Rob bought three books at £4.99 each. What was his change from £20?	Eight stamps of equal value make £4.32. What is the value of each stamp?

£1.80 x 52	£4.32 ÷ 8	£20 - £8.51
£343 ÷ 7	£20 - (3 x £4.99)	(6 x 18p) + (2 x 34p)
£2 x 36	£1.70 x 12	£20 - (4 x £3.57)
(6 x 34p) + (2 x 14p)	£240 ÷ 160	£20 x 1.63

Name_____   ▸ Calculating – Generic Sheet 7

Tricky totals

£5.83	£9.49	£17.55	£14.02
£10.78	£0.61	£22.22	£96.65
£50.30	£41.37	£81.26	£64.71
£93.85	£103.56	£138.29	£154.06
£484.39	£210.99	£292.04	£113.72
£374.63	£568.47	£1000.01	£880.20

PHOTOCOPIABLE
© Hopscotch Educational Publishing 2002

▶ Prices: Level 3

▶ UNIT 3: PRICES
LEVEL 3

🕒 Learning objectives

- To solve problems involving money.
- To find totals, give change and work out which coins to pay.

Key vocabulary

- coin, note, price, cost, change, costs more, more/most expensive, costs less, cheaper, less/least expensive
---

🕒 Resources

- toy money (see Value of Money – Generic Sheet 1, page 28: copy on to stiff card, cut out the coins and notes, then glue heads/tails or front/reverse back to back)

🕒 Introduction

- Start by asking the children how they could pay for items exactly using notes and coins: write a price on the board and ask for suggestions on how to make the amount exactly. Invite several children to come to the front and write different ways on the board. Ask other children to check that the totals are exact by counting out money. Find the way that uses the fewest notes and coins.
- Discuss strategies for finding change by jumping along a blank number line. Let the children practise finding change from both £1 and £5 and count out the necessary coins.

🕒 Activities

- **Activity Sheet 1** – Revise halving strategies during the lesson introduction and reinforce the link between doubling and halving. Encourage the children to check their answers by doubling. As an extension activity, they could cut out the items and take turns to pick two or three and find the total cost.

- **Activity Sheet 2** – Give the children coins to work with and ask them to discuss their answers with a partner to check that they have used the fewest coins possible. As an extension, they could investigate other ways of paying the prices exactly.

- **Activity Sheet 3** – This activity involves working out how to pay using stamps. Explain that the children have only one of each stamp. For many of the parcels there is more than one possible way of paying. Encourage them to list as many ways as they can and discuss their answers with a partner. During the plenary, compile all the possible answers on the board.

- **Activity Sheet 4** – Revise finding change and the key vocabulary. Discuss strategies for working out the answers, for example for questions 1e) and 2e) the words 'less than' reveal that the children should look for the cheaper items on the receipts.

- **Activity Sheet 5** – Encourage the children to explain to a partner how they solved the problems. As an extension, they could write number sentences to show the calculations they used.

- **Activity Sheet 6** – Read the chart with the children and demonstrate how to read it. Point out that the first two questions involve doubling the prices. For question 6, challenge them to find combinations of adults and children which would make a total of £3.60.

🕒 Support

Suggest that the children cut out the stamps for Activity Sheet 3 and find ways to pay for the parcels by putting the stamps in groups.

🕒 Challenge

Set further questions based on the chart in Activity Sheet 6, for example 'Some people buy train tickets. They pay £4.50 in total. Investigate how many people there might be, and to which zone they might be travelling.' Encourage the children to find as many different solutions as they can.

Use Generic Sheet 1 (page 90) for more challenging additions and multiplication

▶ Prices: Level 3

involving prices. Fill in the prices on the price list according to the children's level of attainment. Organise them into groups of four and ask them to each pick a card and work out the total of the items listed. They will need to take care when converting millilitres to litres and working out the price of 18 eggs. They could swap cards and check each other's answers. As an extension, ask them to make more cards showing what other people order from the milkman in one week, and find the totals.

Plenary

Reinforce the key vocabulary by looking at the priced items on Activity Sheet 1 and asking questions about which is the most/least expensive item and whether a particular item is cheaper or more expensive than another.

Display opportunity

Enlarge a menu from a local cafe or takeaway restaurant, or make up a menu with the class showing their favourite foods and drinks with appropriate prices. Ask the children to choose items from the menu and work out the total cost. Ask them what their change from £5 or £10 would be.

Extra activities

Organise the children into small groups and give each group a copy of Generic Sheet 2 (page 91). Ask them to cut out the 'pence cards' and '10p cards' and keep them in separate sets. They should shuffle the sets and take turns to pick a card from each pile to make a two-digit price. They should then say the change from £1, with the others checking the answer is correct. A point can be scored for each correct answer. To practise finding change from £5, the 'pound cards' can be added and the game played again.

Answers

Activity Sheet 1

1. £14 2. £23 3. £15
4. £11 5. £19 6. £45
7. £90 8. £35 9. £150
10. £55 11. £75 12. £500
13. a) £42
    b) £165
    c) £705

Activity Sheet 3

1. 15p, 3p, 2p
2. 21p, 2p OR 15p, 6p, 2p
3. 21p, 3p, 2p OR 15p, 6p, 3p, 2p
4. 27p, 3p OR 21p, 6p, 3p
5. 21p, 15p, 2p OR 27p, 6p, 3p, 2p
6. 34p, 6p, 2p OR 27p, 15p OR 21p, 15p, 6p
7. 27p, 15p, 3p, 2p OR 21p, 15p, 6p, 3p, 2p
8. 34p, 21p, 2p OR 34p, 15p, 6p, 2p
9. 34p, 27p, 6p, 3p, 2p

Activity Sheet 4

1. a) £1.87
   b) Nuts
   c) Doughnut
   d) £1.29
   e) Doughnut, baked beans, samosa
2. a) £10.84
   b) Hand cream
   c) Plasters
   d) £2.73
   e) Plasters, comb, soap

Activity Sheet 5

1. £4.55
2. 90p
3. 15p, 30p, 60p, £1.50
4. 8p
5. £1.03
6. 5

Activity Sheet 6

1. a) 80p   b) £1.50
   c) £1.80 d) £2.90
2. a) £1.20 b) £2.20
   c) £3   d) £4.40
3. £2
4. Zone 4
5. £3.30
6. a) 6   b) 9

Name_____   ▸ Prices – Activity Sheet 1

Half-price sale

Everything in this shop is half price.

Cross out the old price. Write the new price.

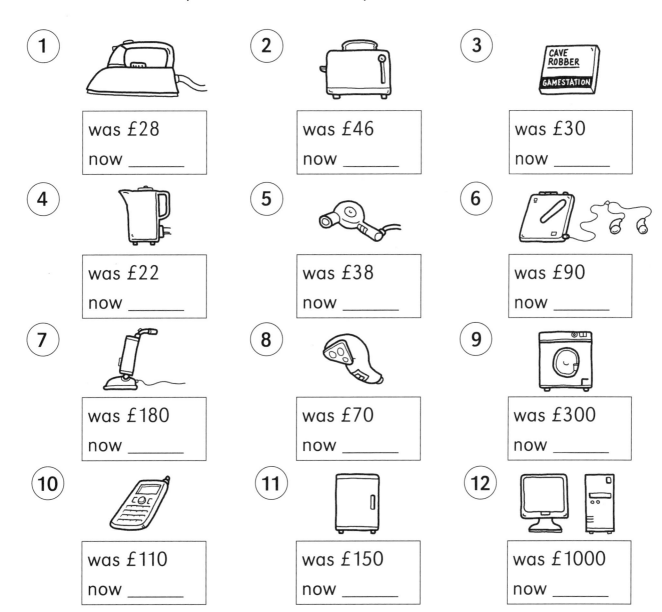

1 was £28   now _____
2 was £46   now _____
3 was £30   now _____
4 was £22   now _____
5 was £38   now _____
6 was £90   now _____
7 was £180 now _____
8 was £70   now _____
9 was £300 now _____
10 was £110 now _____
11 was £150 now _____
12 was £1000 now _____

13   Work out the total cost of these things. Use the new prices.

   a) a toaster and a hairdryer _____

   b) a fridge and a vacuum cleaner _____

   c) a computer, a washing machine and a mobile phone _____

Name_____

▶ Prices – Activity Sheet 2

The fewest coins

How could you pay these amounts exactly, using the fewest coins possible?

List the values of the coins you would use.

29p

43p

34p

_____

_____

_____

58p

76p

63p

_____

_____

_____

91p

87p

99p

_____

_____

_____

_____

_____

_____

£1.14

£1.49

£2.78

_____

_____

_____

_____

_____

_____

68

PHOTOCOPIABLE
© Hopscotch Educational Publishing 2002

Name_____   ▶ Prices – Activity Sheet 3

Stamp prices

You have these stamps.

2p   3p   6p   15p   21p   27p   34p

How can you pay for the postage of these parcels?
List all the different ways you can find.

1 20p

2 23p

3 26p

4 30p

5 38p

6 42p

7 47p

8 57p

9 72p

PHOTOCOPIABLE
© Hopscotch Educational Publishing 2002

Name_____   ▸ Prices – Activity Sheet 4

Shopping receipts

1 a) How much change would you get from £5? _____

   b) Which is the most expensive item? _____

   c) Which is the least expensive item? _____

   d) How much do the nuts and samosa cost altogether? _____

   e) Which three items together cost less than £1.00? Circle the pictures.

Loaf of bread	£0.59
Doughnut	£0.18
Nuts	£0.84
Baked beans	£0.31
Cheese	£0.76
Samosa	£0.45
Total	£3.13

2 a) How much change would you get from £20? _____

   b) Which is the most expensive item? _____

   c) Which is the least expensive item? _____

   d) How much do the shampoo and comb cost altogether? _____

   e) Which three items together cost less than £3.50? Circle the pictures.

Shampoo	£1.65
Toothpaste	£1.59
Plasters	£0.87
Comb	£1.08
Soap	£1.36
Hand cream	£2.61
Total	£9.16

PHOTOCOPIABLE
© Hopscotch Educational Publishing 2002

Name_____   ▸ Prices – Activity Sheet 5

Coffee morning

Alex goes to a coffee morning with her gran. Solve her money problems.

1 It costs 45p to go in. How much change does Alex get from £5?
   _____

2 How much does it cost for both Alex and her gran to go in?
   _____

3 Alex buys a book for her dad from the book stall. She pays exactly with three silver coins all the same value. How much might the book cost?
   _____
   _____

   Work out all the possibilities.

4 She buys four buns at 23p each. How much change does she get from £1? _____

5 She buys some orange juice at 28p, a biscuit at 33p and a coffee for Gran at 42p. How much does she spend? _____

6 At the end of the morning Alex has 80p left. How many raffle tickets could she buy at 15p each? _____

Name_____   ▸ Prices – Activity Sheet 6

Train tickets

The chart shows prices of train tickets from Dunford station to other stations in different zones.

	Prices for travel to:			
	Zone 1	Zone 2	Zone 3	Zone 4
Adult	60p	£1.10	£1.50	£2.20
Child	40p	75p	90p	£1.45

1 How much does it cost for two children to travel to:

   a) Zone 1 _____   b) Zone 2 _____

   c) Zone 3 _____   d) Zone 4 _____

2 How much does it cost for two adults to travel to:

   a) Zone 1 _____   b) Zone 2 _____

   c) Zone 3 _____   d) Zone 4 _____

3 Four children together buy tickets for Zone 2. How much change do they get from £5? _____

4 Three adults are travelling together. Their tickets cost £6.60 in total. Which zone are they going to? _____

5 One adult and two children travel to Zone 3. How much do their tickets cost altogether? _____

6 Some people travel to Zone 1. Their tickets cost £3.60 in total. How many people are there, if they are:

   a) all adults? _____   b) all children? _____

PHOTOCOPIABLE
© Hopscotch Educational Publishing 2002

▶ Prices: Level 4

▶ UNIT 3: PRICES
LEVEL 4

🕒 Learning objectives

- To use all four operations to solve word problems involving money.

Key vocabulary

- costs more, more/most expensive, costs less, cheaper, less/least expensive, discount
---

🕒 Resources

- toy money (see Value of money – Generic Sheet 1, page 28: copy on to stiff card, cut out the coins and notes, then glue heads/tails or front/reverse back to back)
- calculators

🕒 Introduction

- Remind the children of the value of £5, £10 and £20 notes and ensure they can recognise them confidently. Revise finding change from £5, £10 and £20.
- Practise adding and subtracting large amounts of money (up to £1000) and discuss strategies for mental calculation, such as finding units digits which add up to 10 and adding those first. Revise the meaning of 'discount' and practise finding 20% of various prices.

🕒 Activities

- **Activity Sheet 7** – Before beginning the sheet, ask the children to suggest a quick way of multiplying by four, such as doubling and doubling again. Then discuss how to divide by four by halving and halving again. Encourage them to explain to a partner how they solved the problems.

- **Activity Sheet 8** – These problems involve adding two or more prices. The children could check their answers using a calculator. As an extension, ask them to find which three items on the price list make a specified total, for example £23.43 (brakes, saddle, pump).

- **Activity Sheet 9** – Help the children to work out how to solve the problems by putting them into words, for example 'If two birthday cards cost £1.50, how much does one cost?' Explain why it is useful to be able to work out a price per unit in order to be able to compare prices.

- **Activity Sheet 10** – Discuss with the children the fact that it is often more economical to buy larger quantities of goods than to buy in small amounts. Check they understand that in these questions the two women are each buying the same quantity of each item.

- **Activity Sheet 11** – Use this sheet with Generic Sheet 3 (page 92). Ask the children to make a money dice in groups of two or three: they should cut out the template, fold it into a cube along the lines, then spread glue on the tabs and fix them to the inside of the adjacent faces of the cube. They can then take turns to roll the dice and record the coins on their sheet. They will also need real or toy coins (see Value of Money – Generic Sheet 1, page 28).

- **Activity Sheet 12** – Discuss with the children how to carry out a fair test by always comparing like with like. Ask them to think of factors which could distort their results, such as special offers which are on for a limited period only. The activity could be used to find the difference in prices between a small local shop and a large supermarket. Alternatively, the focus could be on the prices of supermarkets' own-brand products. The children could research the prices for homework, or they could use supermarket websites. Suggest that they work in groups of four, two researching 'shop A' and two researching 'shop B'. They can then share their findings when completing the chart. To decide which shop is cheaper overall, they should choose and explain their own methods.

- **Activity Sheet 13** – Encourage the children to use written methods to find the answers and to show their workings clearly. As an extension, 'give' the children a certain amount of money to spend, such as £1200, and ask them what they will buy from the display. Ask them to work out the total and how much change they will receive.

▸ Prices: Level 4

- **Activity Sheet 14** – Encourage the children to explain to a partner how they solved the problems. If they have difficulty working out the cost of 800 g cherries, suggest that they find 800 g as a fraction of 1 kg and then find the equivalent fraction of £5.

Support

Children who find it difficult to divide £.p prices, for example £6.40 ÷ 8, can be encouraged to convert the price into pence and use a written method. Remind them that their answer will be in pence.

Challenge

Once the children have completed Activity Sheet 10, ask them to work out the approximate price per kilogram or price per unit for each woman's purchases and compare the two. Encourage them to round the numbers to enable them to calculate mentally. They could then find an exact answer using a calculator.

To extend Activity Sheet 12, ask the children to research and compare prices of commodities in different parts of Britain, for example house prices and food prices. They could use the Internet for research and/or email pupils at a school in another part of the country and ask them to exchange data. A similar project could be carried out to compare prices in the UK and the USA, focusing on prices of petrol, clothes and food.

Plenary

During the plenary, discuss why some shops are more expensive than others, for example a smaller shop which is in a convenient position and open for longer hours may charge more for goods than a large out-of-town supermarket.

Display opportunity

Make a shop window display based on a shop local to the school. Have items or pictures of items for sale, each with a price tag. Ask questions about the display which involve adding, finding the difference, finding change, multiplying and dividing. Encourage the children to role-play paying for items with the exact money and counting out change.

Extra activities

Use Generic Sheet 4 (page 93) to give practice in finding change. Organise the children into pairs or small groups and give them copies of the sheet to share. Also give them toy money (see Value of Money – Generic Sheet 1, page 28). Ask them to cut out the cards and the spinner and push a pencil through the centre of the spinner. Each child should spin the spinner and take a price card. If the price is less than the value of the note, they should work out the change. If it is more, they should say how much more money is needed to pay the price. Encourage them to show the answer by counting out coins or notes, using the fewest possible.

The cards on Generic Sheet 4 (page 93) can be used for rounding practice. Ask the children to pick a card and round it to the nearest 10p or £1. Remind them that 50p rounds up to the next pound.

Answers

Activity Sheet 7

1. a) £15.20   b) 38p
2. a) £6.15   b) 14
3. a) 64p   b) £5.12   c) £15.36

Activity Sheet 8

1. £22.35
2. a) Yes (£1.03 left over)   b) Yes (98p left over)
   c) No   d) No
   e) Yes (£1.17 left over)
3. £49.37   4. £10.62

Activity Sheet 9

1. a) 75p   b) £1.50   c) 25p   d) 80p
2. a) £1.80   b) £1.24   c) £2.30   d) 82p
3. a) 76p   b) 81p   c) 54p   d) £2

Activity Sheet 10

1. 35p   2. 17p   3. 77p   4. 84p
5. £1.14   6. £3.27

Activity Sheet 13

1. £117   2. £983
3. b) is more expensive
4. b) is cheaper
5. a) £159.80   b) £19.60
   c) £28.60   d) £10.40
   e) £36.80   f) £13

Activity Sheet 14

Sausage rolls	£3.57
Chicken drumsticks	£6.14
Ice creams	£5.12
Lemonade	£4.32
Apples	£1.89
Cherries	£4.00
Bread rolls	£1.35
Balloons	£1.78
Total	£28.17

Change from £30 = £1.83

Four friends

These four children are friends.

Solve the money problems.

1. For Claire's birthday the four children go to see **Aladdin**.

   a) How much do the tickets cost altogether? _____

   b) The children share two bags of sweets. How much do they each pay? _____

2. For Neeraj's birthday the four children go to a theme park.

   a) They pay £24.60 altogether to get in. What is the price per child? _____

   b) Lucy has £3 to spend in the gift shop. How many colouring pens could she buy? _____

3. In the holidays, the four children play tennis together. The price for using the court is £2.56 per hour.

   a) How much does each child pay per hour? _____

   b) The children play for four hours each week. How much does each child spend in two weeks? _____

   c) How much does each child spend in six weeks? _____

▶ Prices – Activity Sheet 8

Second-hand bike

Neil has bought a second-hand bike. He is going to the bike shop with his dad to buy some new parts.

Read the price list.

1. Neil needs a new tyre and new brakes. How much do they cost in total? _____

Price list	
Chain	£5.39
Tyre	£9.49
Saddle	£7.08
Brakes	£12.86
Bell	£1.95
Pump	£3.49
Lock	£5.58

2. He has £12 left. Can he buy these things? If the answer is yes, write how much he would have left over.

   a) a chain and a lock _____

   b) a bell, a pump and a lock _____

   c) a saddle, a bell and a pump _____

   d) a chain, a lock and a bell _____

   e) a bell, a pump and a chain _____

3. Neil bought the bike for £16. He buys a new tyre, new brakes, a bell, a pump and a lock. How much does the bike cost him altogether?
   _____

4. A brand new bike costs £59.99. How much has Neil saved? _____

Name_____   ▸ Prices – Activity Sheet 9

Special offer

1 How much does one of each item cost?

a) 2 for £1.50

cost of one: _____

b) 4 for £6.00

cost of one: _____

c) 5 for £1.25

cost of one: _____

d) 8 for £6.40

cost of one: _____

2 What is the price per kilogram?

a) 2 kg   £3.60

price per kg: _____

b) 10 kg   £12.40

price per kg: _____

c) 0.5 kg   £1.15

price per kg: _____

d) 6 kg   £4.92

price per kg: _____

3 What is the price per litre?

a) 3 litres   £2.28

price per litre: _____

b) 7 litres   £5.67

price per litre: _____

c) 12 litres   £6.48

price per litre: _____

d) 1.5 litres   £3.00

price per litre: _____

PHOTOCOPIABLE
© Hopscotch Educational Publishing 2002

Name_____   ▶ Prices – Activity Sheet 10

Wise buys

Mrs Wise and Mrs Green are neighbours. Work out how much Mrs Wise saved compared with Mrs Green.

1. | Mrs Wise bought | **Price** | Mrs Green bought | **Price** |
|---|---|---|---|
| 1 kg pasta | £1.49 | 2 x 500 g pasta | £0.92 each |

   Mrs Wise saves _____

2. | Mrs Wise bought | **Price** | Mrs Green bought | **Price** |
|---|---|---|---|
| a 4-pack of baked beans | £0.99 | 4 single cans of baked beans | £0.29 each |

   Mrs Wise saves _____

3. | Mrs Wise bought | **Price** | Mrs Green bought | **Price** |
|---|---|---|---|
| 750 g cornflakes | £1.75 | 3 x 250 g cornflakes | £0.84 each |

   Mrs Wise saves _____

4. | Mrs Wise bought | **Price** | Mrs Green bought | **Price** |
|---|---|---|---|
| a 6-pack of cans of cola | £1.74 | 6 single cans of cola | £0.43 each |

   Mrs Wise saves _____

5. | Mrs Wise bought | **Price** | Mrs Green bought | **Price** |
|---|---|---|---|
| a pack of 40 bin liners | £3.22 | 4 packs of 10 bin liners | £1.09 each |

   Mrs Wise saves _____

6. How much did Mrs Wise save in total compared with Mrs Green? _____

PHOTOCOPIABLE
© Hopscotch Educational Publishing 2002

Name_____   ▸ Prices – Activity Sheet 11

Money dice game

Roll a money dice six times. Collect the coins you roll. Record them here.

Use your coins to pay the prices. If you cannot make the price exactly, record how much change you would get.

How to score

Score three points if you make the price exactly.
Score one point if you work out the change correctly.
Score no points if you do not have enough money to pay the price.

Price	Coins used to pay	Change	Points scored
25p			
33p			
8p			
19p			
41p			
12p			
56p			
90p			
£1.01			
62p			
		Total points	

Ask a friend to check your answers. Who scores the most?

Name_____   ▸ Prices – Activity Sheet 12

Price test

Choose two shops near your home or school.
You are going to do a price test to find out which shop is cheaper.

Name of Shop A _____
Name of Shop B _____

Find out the price of all the things on the chart. Complete the chart.

Compare prices for the same size and brand, to make the test fair.

Item	Brand	Weight/ quantity	Price in Shop A	Price in Shop B	Cheaper in A or B?	Difference in price
Tomato ketchup						
Cornflakes						
Loaf of bread						
Crisps						
Box of chocolates						
Carton of juice						
Toothpaste						
Washing up liquid						

Which shop is cheaper overall? _____

PHOTOCOPIABLE
© Hopscotch Educational Publishing 2002

Name_____   ▶ Prices – Activity Sheet 13

Computer shop

Look at the shop display.

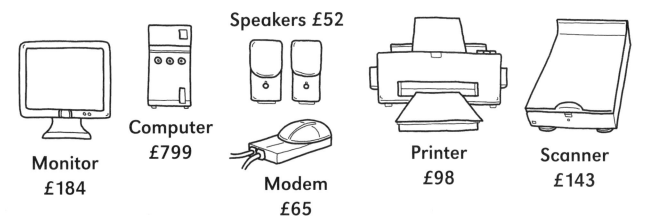

Answer the questions.

1 How much does it cost to buy speakers and a modem?
   _____

2 How much does it cost to buy a computer and
   a monitor? _____

3 Which is more expensive:
       a) a monitor and speakers
   or b) a scanner and a printer?

4 Which is cheaper:
       a) a printer, a modem and speakers
   or b) a scanner and a modem?

Tick a) or b).

5 There is a discount of 20% today. How
   much is the discount on each item?

   a) computer _____   b) printer _____

   c) scanner _____   d) speakers _____

   e) monitor _____   f) modem _____

PHOTOCOPIABLE
© Hopscotch Educational Publishing 2002

Name_____   ▸ Prices – Activity Sheet 14

Shaznay's party

Shaznay is planning a party. Read her shopping list.

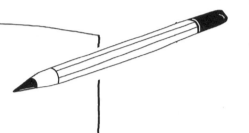

30 sausage rolls
16 chicken drumsticks
12 ice creams
6 litres lemonade
1.5 kg apples
800 g cherries
18 bread rolls
20 balloons

Look at the shop signs. Answer the questions.

10 sausage rolls for £1.19	3 ice creams for £1.28	Lemonade 72p per litre
Apples £1.26 per kg	10 balloons only 89p	Chicken drumsticks 8 for £3.07
Cherries £5.00 per kg		Bread rolls 6 for 45p

How much does Shaznay spend on each item?
Complete the shop receipt.

What is her change from £30? _____

Sausage rolls   _____
Chicken drumsticks   _____
Ice creams   _____
Lemonade   _____
Apples   _____
Cherries   _____
Bread rolls   _____
Balloons   _____
Total   _____

PHOTOCOPIABLE
© Hopscotch Educational Publishing 2002

Prices: Level 5

UNIT 3: PRICES
LEVEL 5

Learning objectives

- To identify and use appropriate operations to solve word problems involving money.
- To read and use prices up to £1 000 000.

Key vocabulary

- costs more, more/most expensive, costs less, cheaper, less/least expensive, discount

Resources

- calculators
- newspapers featuring house prices

Introduction

- Discuss different types of shop offers with the children, for example percentage discounts, money off, 2 for 1 offers and so on. Revise the meaning of 'discount' and practise finding percentage and fraction discounts on various prices.

- Show the children flashcards with large prices (up to £1 000 000). Ask them to read out the prices. Correct any place value errors. Invite ten children to come to the front and give each of them a flashcard. Arrange them in order of value through class discussion. Then show the class large prices in context, for example house prices in a newspaper. Let the children practise writing the prices in words and putting houses in order from least expensive to most expensive.

Activities

- **Activity Sheet 15** – Reinforce the links between percentages, fractions and division, for example 25% is equivalent to a quarter and can be found by dividing by four. Remind the children how to find 10% of a price by dividing by 10, and halving this to find 5%. Show how these can then be added together to give 15%. Point out that in questions 9 and 10 they are given the new price and asked to find the old price. Ask them to think carefully about which number operation they will use.

- **Activity Sheet 16** – Before the children begin the activity sheet, ask them to vote on which shop they think gives the best offer on each product. Write the results on the board. During the plenary, compare this with the actual best offers and discuss how shop offers are worded to make them sound as appealing as possible. For the first question, two shops give the best price per bottle but 'Bargain buys' gives the best offer because the customer needs to buy only one bottle instead of three.

- **Activity Sheet 17** – The children could use a calculator for parts of this activity, or they could use written methods and check their answers on a calculator. Ask them to suggest a quick way of finding the price per year, such as multiplying the monthly price by 2 and by 10 and totalling the two answers. Encourage them to explain their methods to a partner.

- **Activity Sheet 18** – The children could use a calculator for parts of this activity, or they could use written methods and check their answers on a calculator. Remind the children to make sure they work in either pounds or pence, but not a combination of the two within the same calculation.

- **Activity Sheet 19** – This activity provides practice in understanding, adding and subtracting large prices. The children will need newspapers containing house and flat prices within the specified ranges. They can work in pairs or small groups. Alternatively they could research the prices on an estate agent's website. Tell them that it does not matter whether the property is a house or flat.

Support

Change the prices on Activity Sheet 16 to make the calculations less challenging. The price for question 1 could be changed to £1.20 (also change the 'Price slasher' reduction to 36p). The price for question 2 could be changed to £9.00.

▶ Prices: Level 5

🕐 Challenge

Give the children the opportunity to research large prices on the Internet. They could look for prices of cars, long-haul flights and large properties such as castles. Encourage them to write down prices they find in words and figures. They could make comparisons between prices, for example the difference between first class and economy class flights or the difference between buying a car in Britain and abroad (emphasise the importance of finding prices for a car of identical age, make and model in order to make a fair comparison).

🕐 Plenary

Invite children who have researched large prices on the Internet or in newspapers to share their findings with the rest of the class. Write some of the prices on the board and ask questions to reinforce place value. Create word problems from the prices for the children to solve using addition, subtraction, multiplication or division.

🕐 Display opportunity

Encourage the children to look for prices in everyday life and to bring in adverts, newspapers and leaflets featuring large prices. Display the prices in order of value and ask questions for the children to solve.

🕐 Extra activities

Use Generic Sheet 5 (page 94) for practice in recognising and ordering prices up to £1 000 000. Organise the children into pairs and ask them to cut out the cards and write each price in words on the back of the card. Then challenge them to put the cards in order of value, looking only at the digit sides. When they have decided on the correct order, they can check they are correct by looking at the prices in words.

Write quantities on the receipts on Generic Sheet 6 (page 95) to suit the children's level of attainment, for example 3 kg, 2.2 kg, 400 g. Ask them to work out the cost of each item and fill in the total.

🕐 Answers

Activity Sheet 15

1. £6.15
   £18.45
2. £4.70
   £14.10
3. £20.60
   £61.80
4. £26.25
   £78.75
5. £4.50
   £25.50
6. £7.20
   £40.80
7. £16.50
   £93.50
8. £10.80
   £61.20
9. £52.98
10. £35.64

Activity Sheet 16

1. Price slasher   £1.13
   Discount store   £1.22
   Save-a-lot   £1.08
   Bargain buys   £1.08
2. Price slasher   £5.30
   Discount store   £4.68
   Save-a-lot   £5.85
   Bargain buys   £5.20

Activity Sheet 17

1. a) £34.40
   b) £412.80
   c) £8.60
   d) £103.20
2. a) £37.80
   b) £453.60
   c) £12.60
   d) £151.20

Activity Sheet 18

1. a) £3.60
   b) £14.40
   c) £18.72
   d) £30.24
2. 40 litres
3. 7.5 miles
4.

Journey distance	Number of litres needed	Price per litre	Cost of journey
90 miles	12 litres	72p	£8.64
165 miles	22 litres	72p	£15.84
120 miles	16 litres	72p	£11.52
225 miles	30 litres	72p	£21.60

Name_____ ▸ Prices – Activity Sheet 15

Clothes sale

These clothes have 25% discount. Find the new prices.

1  old price £24.60   2   old price £18.80
                       discount   £_____   discount   £_____
                       new price £_____   new price £_____

3  old price £82.40   4   old price £105.00
                       discount   £_____   discount   £_____
                       new price £_____   new price £_____

These clothes have 15% discount. Find the new prices.

5  old price £30.00   6  old price £48.00
                       discount   £_____   discount   £_____
                       new price £_____   new price £_____

7   old price £110.00   8  old price £72.00
                       discount   £_____   discount   £_____
                       new price £_____   new price £_____

These clothes have 50% discount. Read the new prices. Work out the old prices.

9   old price £_____   10   old price £_____
                       new price £26.49   new price £17.82

PHOTOCOPIABLE
© Hopscotch Educational Publishing 2002

Name_____   ▶ Prices – Activity Sheet 16

A good offer?

Work out the price per item in each shop. Find out which shop gives the best offer.

1 Silky shampoo
   Usual price £1.62

Some of the prices might work out the same.

Shop	Offer	Price per bottle	Tick the best offer
Price slasher	49p off		
Discount store	25% discount		
Save-a-lot	3 for the price of 2		
Bargain buys	$\frac{1}{3}$ off		

2 Protector sun lotion
   Usual price £7.80

Shop	Offer	Price per tube	Tick the best offer
Price slasher	£2.50 off		
Discount store	40% discount		
Save-a-lot	buy one and get another half price		
Bargain buys	$\frac{1}{3}$ off		

PHOTOCOPIABLE
© Hopscotch Educational Publishing 2002

Name_____   ▸ Prices – Activity Sheet 17

Digital prices

Jenny and Sam's family are looking at prices for digital television. Look at the price chart.

Package	Price per month	Extra channels	Price per month
A	£33.60	Cartoons	£4.90
B	£31.90	Football	£5.90
C	£29.30	Music	£5.10
D	£26.70	Arts	£4.40

1 Jenny wants to get package C plus the music channel.

   a) How much is this per month? _____

   b) How much is this per year? _____

   Jenny has offered to pay a quarter of the cost with her pocket money.

   c) How much will she pay per month? _____

   d) How much will she pay per year? _____

2 Sam wants to get package B plus the football channel.

   a) How much is this per month? _____

   b) How much is this per year? _____

   Sam has offered to pay a third of the cost with his pocket money.

   c) How much will he pay per month? _____

   d) How much will he pay per year? _____

Name _____   ▸ Prices – Activity Sheet 18

Petrol puzzles

The price of petrol is 72p per litre.

1   What is the cost of:

   a) 5 litres? _____

   b) 20 litres? _____

   c) 26 litres? _____

   d) 42 litres? _____

Write your answers in pounds.

2   Miss Heyes fills her tank from empty. She pays £28.80. How many litres does her tank hold?

   _____

3   Miss Heyes travels 150 miles. She uses half the tank of petrol. How many miles does she travel for each litre of petrol? _____

4   Use the answer to question 3 to help you complete the chart.

Journey distance	Number of litres needed	Price per litre	Cost of journey
90 miles		72p	
	22	72p	
120 miles		72p	
		72p	£21.60

PHOTOCOPIABLE
© Hopscotch Educational Publishing 2002

Name_____   ▶ Prices – Activity Sheet 19

House prices

Look on the Internet or in newspapers for house prices.
Find prices to write in the blanks.

House A
Find a house price less than £100 000.
_____

House B
Find a house price between £100 001 and £170 000.
_____

House C
Find a house price between £170 001 and £250 000.
_____

House D
Find a house price more than £250 000.
_____

Answer the questions.

1   Write the price of House A in words.
    _____

2   Write the price of House D in words.
    _____

3   What is the difference in price between House A and House B?
    _____

4   What is the difference in price between House B and House D?
    _____

5   Write the total price of House B and House C.
    _____

PHOTOCOPIABLE
© Hopscotch Educational Publishing 2002

Name_____ ▸ Prices – Generic Sheet 1

Milk round

Price list

Milk (1 pint) _____

Orange juice (1 pint) _____

Cream (500 ml) _____

Eggs (half dozen) _____

Potatoes (2.5 kg) _____

Mrs Gupta

8 pts milk _____

1 litre cream _____

1 dozen eggs _____

Total _____

Mr Robinson

5 pts milk _____

2 pts orange juice _____

2.5 kg potatoes _____

Total _____

Ms Kerr

7 pts milk _____

3 pts orange juice _____

2 litres cream _____

2.5 kg potatoes _____

Total _____

Mr Harris

9 pts milk _____

500 ml cream _____

18 eggs _____

5 kg potatoes _____

Total _____

PHOTOCOPIABLE
© Hopscotch Educational Publishing 2002

Name_____   ▶ Prices – Generic Sheet 2

Digit cards

Pence cards

0	1	2	3	4
5	6	7	8	9

10p cards

0	1	2	3	4
5	6	7	8	9

Pound cards

0	1	2	3	4

PHOTOCOPIABLE
© Hopscotch Educational Publishing 2002

Money dice

Price cards

£1.31	£4.89	£5.99	£0.67
£8.89	£10.60	£13.01	£15.15
£9.99	£2.61	£19.50	£3.45
£34.85	£1.99	£6.77	£48.20
£22.56	£8.98		
£3.43	£20.24		
£16.72	£25.02		

Large prices

£1080	£167 000	£210 000	£6800
£21 500	£945 000	£55 000	£328 000
£3840	£500 001	£76 600	£241 600
£986	£99 990	£4671	£101 010
£800 022	£310 000	£92 000	£7220
£2393	£601	£100 000	£60 000

Name_____   ▸ Prices – Generic Sheet 6

Weigh it up

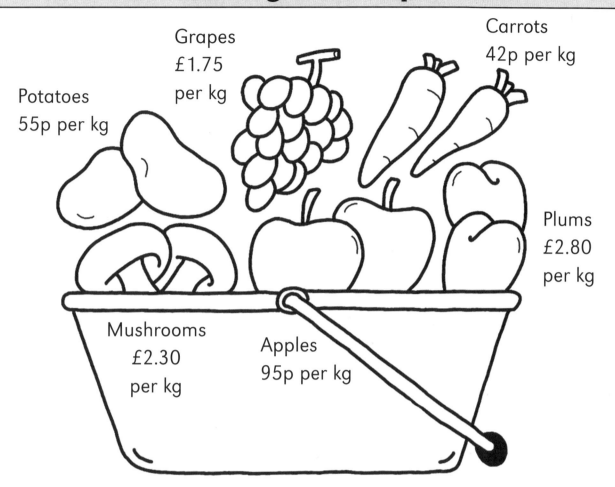

Potatoes 55p per kg
Grapes £1.75 per kg
Carrots 42p per kg
Plums £2.80 per kg
Mushrooms £2.30 per kg
Apples 95p per kg

Receipt

Item and quantity	Price
_____ mushrooms	_____
_____ potatoes	_____
_____ grapes	_____
_____ carrots	_____
_____ apples	_____
_____ plums	_____
Total	_____

Receipt

Item and quantity	Price
_____ mushrooms	_____
_____ potatoes	_____
_____ grapes	_____
_____ carrots	_____
_____ apples	_____
_____ plums	_____
Total	_____

PHOTOCOPIABLE
© Hopscotch Educational Publishing 2002

My Assessment Sheet

Name: _____ Date: _____

Main learning objective: _____

_____

(teacher to fill in before copying)

I can do this work: with support ☐

                       independently ☐

                       with an extension ☐

I have learned to _____

_____

Favourite activity
I really enjoyed _____

_____

Most challenging activity
I need more practice in _____

_____

My next target
I want to get better at _____

_____

PHOTOCOPIABLE
© Hopscotch Educational Publishing 2002